Summer Sermons,
Winter Thoughts

Summer Sermons, Winter Thoughts

PETER C. HODGSON

CASCADE *Books* • Eugene, Oregon

SUMMER SERMONS, WINTER THOUGHTS

Copyright © 2018 Peter C. Hodgson. All rights reserved. Except for brief quotations in critical publications or reviews, no part of this book may be reproduced in any manner without prior written permission from the publisher. Write: Permissions, Wipf and Stock Publishers, 199 W. 8th Ave., Suite 3, Eugene, OR 97401.

Cascade Books
An Imprint of Wipf and Stock Publishers
199 W. 8th Ave., Suite 3
Eugene, OR 97401

www.wipfandstock.com

PAPERBACK ISBN: 978-1-5326-4705-5
HARDCOVER ISBN: 978-1-5326-4706-2
EBOOK ISBN: 978-1-5326-4707-9

Cataloging-in-Publication data:

Names: Hodgson, Peter Crafts, 1934-, author.
Title: Summer sermons, winter thoughts / Peter C. Hodgson.
Description: Eugene, OR: Cascade Books, 2018. | Includes bibliographical references and index.
Identifiers: ISBN: 978-1-5326-4705-5 (paperback). | ISBN: 978-1-5326-4706-2 (hardcover). | ISBN: 978-1-5326-4707-9 (ebook).
Subjects: LCSH: Theology. | Sermons, American—21st Century. | Sermons, American—Pennsylvania. | Presbyterian Church—United States—Sermons.
Classification: BX9886 H63 2018 (paperback). | BX9886 (ebook).

Manufactured in the U.S.A.   05/22/18

Scripture quotations are from New Revised Standard Version Bible, copyright © 1989 National Council of the Churches of Christ in the United States of America. Used by permission. All rights reserved worldwide

Contents

Preface | vii

Part 1: Summer Sermons
    Eagles Mere Presbyterian Church
1 July 11, 2003—In Remembrance of Jack Edward Hodgson | 3
2 July 15, 2006—In Remembrance of Charles P. Deloache | 7
3 July 1, 2007—Let Freedom Ring | 10
4 July, 2010—Excursions into Difficulty | 16
5 August 28, 2011—Wind | 24
6 June 28, 2015—Your Faith Has Made You Well | 28
7 May 27, 2016—Audacity and Humility | 34
    Princeton University Chapel
8 August 14, 2016—Hearing | 38
9 September 3, 2017—Feet | 42
10 July 22, 2018—Abba | 47

Part 2: Winter Thoughts
11 Lives | 55
12 Theologies | 74
13 Politics | 106

Writings by Peter C. Hodgson | 117
Bibliography | 123
Index | 127

Preface

Eagles Mere is a village in Northeastern Pennsylvania, located between two branches of the Susquehanna River: the north branch, which runs through Scranton Wilkes-Barre, and the west branch, which flows past Williamsport. Eagles Mere itself, the lake, in the Sullivan Highlands, has an elevation of two thousand feet and is one of the highest natural lakes in the eastern United States. Eagles Mere the village became a resort community in the latter part of the nineteenth century with the construction of hotels and cottages. Eagles Mere Park, at the north end of the lake, started out as a Chautauqua. The cottages survive, and many new ones have been built, so the population swells from two hundred to over three thousand in the summer. The story of how my family and I came to this place will be told later. The town has four churches: Catholic, community, Episcopal, and Presbyterian. Only the community church is open the year round. The others are seasonal and run programs during the summer months. The Presbyterian church was built in 1887 from stones of a demolished barn and celebrated its 130th anniversary in 2017. In recent years (since my retirement in 2003) I have preached several times in this church. These summer sermons are collected here, plus one for a memorial service at my college. The church is pictured on the front cover.

People ask, when they first see you at the beginning of a new season in Eagles Mere, how your winter has been. By "winter" they mean the whole time that has elapsed since the previous summer, so winter can last up to ten months. For Eva and me,

Preface

"winter" means Nashville, Tennessee, and lasts about eight and a half months. We live in Nashville because I taught at Vanderbilt University Divinity School. As befits the season, winter thoughts should be longer (and darker) than summer sermons. At least that's what I thought when I began writing them. They represent brief autobiographical reflections on lives, theologies, and politics.

Most of the sermons (following the "remembrances") are based on biblical texts, but two are not. "Excursions into Difficulty" draws upon a novel by Marilynne Robinson, and "Audacity and Humility" has a more secular setting; both, however, include biblical references. I think preachers make a mistake if they rely only on biblical texts. A wealth of literature is available to them, including the great thinkers of the church and writers of fiction and poetry with deep insight into the human condition. Congregations need to learn about these resources. Why not preach a sermon based on Augustine's *Confessions* or George Eliot's *Middlemarch* or Dietrich Bonhoeffer's *Letters and Papers from Prison*? Scripture is special: it is the foundational document of Christianity, but it is not everything. An amazing tradition follows in its wake.

The combination of summer sermons and winter thoughts is strange to say the least, but the whole is loosely held together by an underlying question: how is God efficaciously present in history without violating the fabric of history? This question is addressed in various ways in two distinct genres, the use of which is for me a new venture.

Lakes have played an important role in my life and in Eva's life—not only Eagles Mere Lake, but also Magician Lake in Michigan during my childhood, Lake Michigan and Stony Lake during my camping years, Lake Balaton in Hungary during Eva's childhood, Sebago Lake in Maine where we first met, and Percy Priest Lake near Nashville where I sailed for many years. I continue to sail during the summers on the Lake of the Eagles, and sailing has become for me a metaphor of theology.

PART 1

Summer Sermons

Eagles Mere Presbyterian Church

1

JULY 11, 2003

In Remembrance of Jack Edward Hodgson

December 11, 1907—May 26, 2003

My father, Jack Hodgson, was born in Maywood, Illinois, December 11, 1907, the second of three sons of William Welch Hodgson and Alice Jennings Hodgson. I have to report that already his birth caused a controversy. He was christened John George Hodgson III, after his grandfather. His uncle was John George Hodgson II, and later this uncle had a son whom *he* named John George III. Now there were two John George Hodgsons III. This so upset his father (who thought he had an agreement with his brother about naming rights) that my father's name was changed to Jack Edward Hodgson. So that's how he became "Jack."

The grandfather, John George Hodgson, came to the United States from England when he was a small boy. His parents, John and Margaret Hodgson, immigrated to Philadelphia in the early 1850s where John set up business as a tailor and merchant. When my family started coming to Eagles Mere in 1957, we were (without realizing it at the time) returning to the state of our ancestors.

Part 1: Summer Sermons

John George proved to be very gifted mechanically and, after moving to Chicago, invented much of the equipment that was used to make tin cans. He was closely associated with the founders of the American Can Company and the Continental Can Company. My father followed in the footsteps of his father and grandfather when he went to work for Continental Can in 1931, sweeping out boxcars.

In 1940 my father became manager of the Continental Can plant in Memphis. He was transferred to St. Louis in 1948 and to Baltimore in 1950, where he managed the old Tin Deco plant until his retirement in 1965. I worked in the plant for a couple of summers and learned how much my father was revered by the employees. Every morning he would make a round of the plant, speaking with the workers. Many of them came to him for personal advice and counsel. He was more like a pastor to them than a boss, and that plant was his parish. As a result this was one of the most efficient operations in the Continental system. The Tin Deco plant was unique. It didn't make ordinary tin cans but specialty products out of tinplate, such as waste cans, trays, bread baskets, and aspirin containers. The plant became famous for its Decoware line. My father still had his Decoware waste cans. He didn't think much of the plastic products that put Tin Deco out of business.

When my father retired in 1965, he earned a master's degree in business administration and taught part-time at the University of Baltimore, where he proved to be a popular teacher, until 1983. Teaching, I think, had always been his secret ambition. Also in 1966, he and my mother purchased the Mushroom Cottage in Eagles Mere Park, and spent every summer there until her death in 1993. Since then Eva and I spent summers with him in the cottage up through last summer. Now we continue on our own.

In high school my father was a star athlete, excelling in football, track, and swimming. In his senior year at Oak Park High School, he was expelled along with a number of other boys for having joined a forbidden fraternity. So his last year of high school was at Princeton Prep, then he went to Northwestern and the University of Michigan. Later he played tennis and golf. He became an

In Remembrance of Jack Edward Hodgson

excellent golfer and in 1968 won the Eagles Mere Country Club championship. He shot a hole in one and was senior champion on more than one occasion. He continued playing golf until a few years ago. He also loved to read, talk, and debate. He expressed his opinions candidly, and had a wonderful sense of humor. He affected the lives of many people.

My father's contributions to Eagles Mere were numerous. He helped organize the Eagles Mere Park Association, which won the rights (through legendary legal battles) to the land and the roads in the Park, and for many years he was a leader in the Association. He, Bud Hockley, Charles Bidelspacher, Charley Brogan, and Arch Houstle were a formidable team. My father also played an important role at the Country Club, serving in various official roles and creating some of the tournaments that are still played.

His last few years were spent at Oak Crest Village in Baltimore, where he won the affection of all who knew him. He befriended in particular one lonely man. His love of life and the courage with which he endured his final illness struck a responsive chord with the staff, which went beyond the call of duty to help him.

In the passage I read from the Gospel of John, we are told that when Martha learned that Jesus was coming she went to meet him while Mary stayed at home. Yet it was the quiet devotion and sorrow of Mary that led Jesus to call her brother out from the dead. I have always thought my mother was like the Mary of this story (though she had some of Martha's qualities too).[1] In any event, my father was moved by his Mary to do things he would not otherwise have done. She made him a better person, and he missed her sorely when she died ten years ago this August. At her memorial service here in Eagles Mere, he made some remarks. At the end he said simply, "Life must go on."

---

1. On the occasion of my parents' fiftieth wedding anniversary in 1982, Paul Kaminski, husband of my cousin Julie, made an acronym out of her name. M is for "matriarch," A is for "adventurous," R is for "rigorous," and Y is for "youthful." That sums her up well.

Part 1: Summer Sermons

Several years ago my father prepared an album of photos of his youth and family and a brief résumé of his life. He wrote a statement to go into the album. I'll conclude by reading part of it:

"This album contains no pictures of, nor does it express any of my religious experiences through my grammar, high school, and college years. Yet, religion influenced my life more than almost any other activity that I encountered.

"I was brought up in an Episcopal Church in Oak Park, Illinois. This was a *high* church that adhered to all the ritual and form, I guess, of the Catholic Church. I was confirmed in this church, but much more I sang in the Boy's Choir, which meant that I attended not only Sunday School every Sunday but also church. During high school I was an acolyte, that is, I attended the priest during the service when we had Communion, which was often, and especially during the holidays. I only mention this as I was a one-hundred-percent Christian. But this changed.

"During college I took not only science but history courses. I learned what the Christians did to the non-Christians and others, as well as to Copernicus, to Vesalius who discovered the circulation of blood, and to those who stood in the way of the Crusades, which killed thousands looking for the Holy Grail. I left college a different person. But I was still a Christian.

"Now I mention something quite confidential. My mother had it, I have it, my grandson has it, no other member of my family has it. What is it? It is an inner sense of being, of feeling, of sensing the unknown, of others.

"Yes, my life has been affected by religion."

—Jack Hodgson, August 7, 1997

2

July 15, 2006

In Remembrance of Charles P. Deloache

November 24, 1924—February 23, 2006

Thirteen years ago here at Eagles Mere something happened that tells a lot about Charles DeLoache. My father had gone for the mail, and when he returned to the cottage he found my mother lying on the floor, gasping "I'm leaving you, Jack." The only thing he could think to do was to call Charlie (the number, he told me, was very easy to remember). Charlie and Marge came right over. When they saw my mother, they called an ambulance and made her as comfortable as possible. Charlie drove my father to the Muncy Valley Hospital and stayed with him the rest of that long and difficult day. A few days later he and Marge drove to Baltimore for the funeral, and for the next few months they provided a lot of comfort for my father.

Now Charlie has died, unexpectedly, like my mother, and before his time. Those who knew him well grieve his loss, and our thoughts and prayers go out to Marge, Bill and Phil and their families. Charlie and Marge were high school sweethearts, and they

Part 1: Summer Sermons

spent over three-quarters of their lives together. That's an amazing accomplishment. They shared their love of golf, Florida, Eagles Mere, good wine and good music. They were good for each other. I noticed that Marge sometimes had a calming effect when Charlie got carried away in a political discussion.

My parents met Charlie and Marge many years ago at the Baltimore Symphony. They had season tickets adjacent to each other, and after a number of concerts they had become well-acquainted. Knowing their shared passion for golf, my father told Charlie and Marge about a little resort in the mountains of northeastern Pennsylvania with a wonderful golf course. The DeLoaches started coming to Eagles Mere in 1972 and in a few years they purchased the Greenwoods on Forest Avenue. For the next thirty years my father and Charlie were close golfing buddies.

Living alone was not easy for my father after my mother's death, and the DeLoaches tried to keep him busy and out of trouble in Baltimore. In 1997 he suffered a mild stroke, and again the first thing he did was to call Charlie, who took him to the hospital and stayed with him until I could arrive. My father once told me that Charlie was the only one of his old friends who had not abandoned him (of course most of his old friends had passed away by then). His last year was difficult, and Charlie spent as much time as he could with him during the last week of his life. They had great admiration and affection for each other. Now they are both gone.

Charlie was a loyal son of Scotland. His family owned a castle, somewhere in the vicinity of Aberdeen, and he loved to visit there and to play golf in the country where the game was invented. Charlie is the only person who did not show signs of boredom with my slides of Scotland. In fact he loved them, and because of his enthusiasm he and Marge were subjected to viewings on other topics. We are pleased that a piper could come from the St. Andrew's Society, and we thought it would be appropriate to include part of the Scots Confession in this service. While the words are not the easiest to say in unison, I think Charlie would approve them.

> We confess and acknowledge one God alone, to whom alone we must cleave, whom alone we must serve, whom

In Remembrance of Charles P. Deloache

alone we must worship, and in whom alone we put our trust. Who is eternal, infinite, immeasurable, incomprehensible, omnipotent, invisible; one in substance and yet distinct in three persons, the Father, the Son, and the Holy Spirit. By whom we confess and believe all things in heaven and earth, visible and invisible, to have been created, to be retained in their being, and to be ruled and guided by his inscrutable providence for such end as his eternal wisdom, goodness, and justice have appointed, and to the manifestation of his glory.

3

July 1, 2007

Let Freedom Ring

Luke 4:14–21

In 1963 Martin Luther King Jr. wrote an open letter from the Birmingham city jail in which he responded to criticisms of the civil rights movement by white moderates. He concluded that it was not so bad to be called an "extremist." Was not Jesus an extremist for love? Or Amos an extremist for justice? Or Paul for the Christian gospel? Then King asked, Was not Martin Luther an extremist? Think of his famous words, "Here I stand; I cannot do otherwise, so help me God."

King and his namesake were both extremists in the cause of freedom—freedom of conscience, religion, faith, life itself. On this Sunday before our great American celebration of freedom, it would be well to reflect on Martin Luther and Martin Luther King. Now, I suspect that with the mention of Martin Luther some of you are thinking that I'm experiencing some identity-confusion. No, I am not Jack Clark,[1] even though my sermon title has three

---

1. The Reverend John Clark, retired Lutheran minister, summer resident of Eagles Mere, and frequent preacher at the Eagles Mere Presbyterian Church. His sermon titles always had three words. I substituted for him this summer.

words, and even though I am proposing to talk about Luther. The Eagles Mere Presbyterian Church always welcomes Jack, and Presbyterians should keep in mind that without Luther there would have been no Reformation and thus no Presbyterianism.

In 1520 Luther published a treatise that became the hallmark of the Reformation, called *The Freedom of a Christian* (*De Libertate Christiana*—that would have worked as a sermon title too). He sent it to Pope Leo X along with an open letter—a letter written by a still-obscure monk who clearly had been liberated from bondage to authority and felt free to speak the truth to power. He addressed the pope as an equal and offered advice liberally. He remarked that all Christians are servants of Christ (the pope being merely "the servant of servants"), and he implied that the only true authority is that of scripture, reason, and conscience. He employed a good deal of satire and mockery. It is hard to imagine such a letter being written even today, say by a young pastor to his presbytery or bishop, or by an employee to her CEO. A couple of years before the treatise, Luther had changed the spelling of his name from Luder to Luther. He discovered within his new name the Greek word for freedom, *eleutheria*, and sometimes he signed his letters as Eleutherius, "the free one."

The Freedom of a Christian sets forth two famous theses: "A Christian is a perfectly free lord of all, subject to none." "A Christian is a perfectly dutiful servant of all, subject to all." The first thesis means that the Word of God alone gives freedom, liberating us from earthly lords, human institutions, and works required for salvation. The gift is unlimited and universal, but it must be inwardly appropriated: all that is needed is the faith by which God's Word is believed, accepted, trusted. This faith is more than a verbal thing; it entails an actual participation in Christ, like the iron that glows in fire. Faith unites the soul with Christ as a bride to her bridegroom; they become one flesh, a marriage of God and humanity in which God's freedom becomes humanity's freedom.

The second thesis had several meanings for Luther. The most important one is that a Christian does not live for him- or herself alone but all people on earth. We are called to live a life for

Part 1: Summer Sermons

others, not for ourselves. Free from works as a means of salvation, or as merits that deserve rewards, we should, like Christ, empty ourselves and become servants of all, making our works a gift to others. Luther also said that being a dutiful servant meant that Christians are subject to the governing authorities and should stay in their own profession and station in life. For the sake of peace and order, they should not disrupt the social fabric or oppose unjust and violent tyrants unless the latter demand something contrary to God. The freedom of a Christian applies principally to the inner, spiritual kingdom, not to the external, worldly kingdom. Now this seems to be an advocacy of patriotism, which in itself is a good thing. But are not injustice and violence contrary to God's will? If our founding fathers had not opposed an unjust and violent tyrant, our nation would not have been born. If Martin Luther King had not opposed an unjust and violent social order, the American dream of freedom would for many of its citizens still be a nightmare. Sometimes patriotism requires going against the established order of things.

Let us turn our attention to Martin Luther King. The story of how he came by his name is fascinating. Just as Luther himself changed his name, so also did King's father, Martin Luther King Sr. In accord with the wish of his mother he was baptized Michael, after the archangel; but his father had preferred the names of his two brothers, Martin and Luther. As Michael became a young man, he began to change his name. First he called himself Michael Luther King; then in 1934, after a visit to Germany, he changed it to Martin Luther King. By this time he was the pastor of a prominent Atlanta church, and the name seemed suitable. His eldest son, born in 1929, was baptized Michael King Jr. But in elementary school he was called Martin or M. L., and in 1957 his birth certificate was altered to Martin Luther King Jr. It is as though providence were preparing a name for a great leader.

A linkage to the Reformers was present in the consciousness of the black church. Martin Luther could be seen as the Moses of Protestantism, leading his people out of Babylonian captivity to the Roman church. Martin Luther King Jr. became the Moses of the civil rights movement, leading his people out of bondage to segregation and racism. Martin Luther needed Martin Luther King to correct and concretize his own vision of freedom. Martin Luther King benefited from the name of Martin Luther: it conveyed his prophetic role, lent him authority as a religious and political leader, and in a hidden way linked him with the biblical word for freedom.

King was not simply a disciple of Martin Luther. He was critical of the view shared by Luther and Calvin that God is as an absolute sovereign who predestines some to salvation and others to damnation. He recognized that inner freedom cannot flourish in the context of external bondage, and thus he challenged Luther's division between two kingdoms, spiritual and worldly. He adhered rather to the words that Jesus read from the prophet Isaiah concerning good news for the poor, release of captives, recovery of sight for the blind, and liberation of the oppressed. He extended Luther's vision of the freedom of a Christian to include all of God's children, not just Christians. And he gave concrete meaning to Luther's idea of a life of service on behalf of others.

He became an advocate of nonviolent resistance as the means of achieving not merely desegregation but integration. He said that we do not want a society where people are "physically desegregated and spiritually segregated, where elbows are together and hearts are apart." He knew that desegregation would be relatively easy to obtain and enforce, but that integration was a long, distant, and unenforceable goal because it involves an inward transformation: something must touch the hearts and souls of human beings and bring them together spiritually. He described three preconditions of integration. First, there must be a recognition of the sacredness of human personality. This recognition is deeply rooted in both our religious and our political heritage. The Hebraic-Christian tradition expresses it with the conviction that *every* human being is created in the image of God, that this image is universally shared in equal portion by every person, that there is no graded scale of essential worth. The same truth is affirmed by the Declaration of Independence. Second, there must be a recognition that freedom entails the capacity to deliberate, choose, and respond. Without such freedom, life itself is shackled and destroyed. The system of slavery and later segregation wreaked havoc on black people for generations by constricting this freedom. Finally, there must be a recognition of the solidarity of the human family. Integration is the goal because we basically are all one: God has made of one blood all nations. Humans are social creatures, engaged from the beginning of civilization in the great adventure of community. The self cannot be a self without other selves; all human beings are caught up in a network of mutuality. King envisioned this mutuality as a beloved community and a free community.

He described this community in his most famous speech, the keynote address for the March on Washington in August 1963. Despite shameful conditions and the many difficulties that lie ahead, King said, "I still have a dream—a dream deeply rooted in the American dream that one day this nation will rise up and live out the true meaning of its creed." This will be the day when all of God's children will be able to sing with new meaning the words of the hymn, "My Country 'Tis of Thee"—words that end with the appeal to "let freedom ring" from every mountainside. King echoed these words in a great refrain: let freedom ring from the mighty mountains of New York and the heightening Alleghenies of Pennsylvania all the way down to Stone Mountain of Georgia, Lookout Mountain of Tennessee, and every hill and molehill of Mississippi. Then he concluded, "When we allow freedom to ring, when we let it ring from every village and hamlet, from every state and city, we will be able to speed up that day when all of God's children—black men and white men, Jews and Gentiles, Catholic and Protestants—will be able to join hands and to sing in the words of the old Negro spiritual, 'Free at last, free at last; thank God Almighty, we are free at last.'"

Well, *our* little mountain is in "the heightening Alleghenies of Pennsylvania." As we prepare to celebrate this Independence Day—to hear once again those great words about equality and the right to life, liberty, and the pursuit of happiness—let us reflect on Martin Luther and Martin Luther King and on what their legacy means in our particular time and place. We come to this mountaintop for respite and relaxation, but we know that the problems of the world can't be left behind for long. Conditions as shameful as those that King described in 1963 are still with us, but in different forms. Integration hasn't really taken hold in America. The gap between wealth and poverty has widened. Millions lack basic medical care. Immigrants struggle for basic human rights. Polarizing conflicts over values have divided the nation. The fear of terrorism has driven policies that are tragically counterproductive. Freedom is sacrificed in its defense. Ethnic and religious hatreds have escalated throughout the world. The beloved community seems far away, not only as a national community but also as a global community. Today more than ever we need the courage of Martin Luther and the vision of Martin Luther King. Here I stand—I have a dream—Let freedom ring!

4

July, 2010

Excursions into Difficulty

One of the most imaginative theological minds at work today is that of the novelist Marilynne Robinson. Her interlinked novels, *Gilead* (2004) and *Home* (2008),[1] provide a wealth of figures, images, and narratives for those who are interested in theological and pastoral issues. Far from the caricatures that have become standard in American literature and culture, Robinson offers a sympathetic and complex portrait of one minister-theologian in particular, John Ames.

In 1956 (the time-setting for the novels) Ames is seventy-six-years old and still pastor of the Congregational church in Gilead, Iowa. The name Gilead is familiar to us from the Hebrew Bible, where it refers to a hilly area east of the Jordan River, famous for the resin from a tree used for medicinal purposes. In his lament

---

1. *Gilead*, winner of the Pulitzer Prize, was published in 2004; and *Home*, winner of the Orange Prize, was published in 2008. The novels are unusual in that they tell an overlapping story from different perspectives. I refer to an interview with Marilynne Robinson conducted by *Religion & Ethics Newsweekly* on March 18, 2005 (pbs.org./wnet/religionandethics/week829/interview.html). Robinson teaches at the University of Iowa Writers' Workshop. She is also the author of *Housekeeping* and has published three works of nonfiction.

for Israel, the Lord asks, "Is there no balm in Gilead? Is there no physician there?" (Jeremiah 8:22). The question posed by the novels is whether a *home* can be found in Gilead—the fictional Gilead being a small town in western Iowa founded by abolitionists in the nineteenth century as an outpost in the struggle over whether Kansas would enter the union as a slave or a free state.

Gilead takes the form of an extended letter written by Ames to his six-year-old son Robby, a letter that he hopes the boy will read when he has grown up and his father is long gone from this world. Ames writes with both grief and joy—emotions that seem to be built into each other when a man fathers a child at age sixty-nine. Ames's first wife died in childbirth, and the baby girl with her. For nearly fifty years of his ministry Ames lived alone, until a young woman he had never seen before appeared at his church one day—a woman of mysterious background (a "Mary Magdalene") with a sadness and intensity of expression, and a beauty and simplicity of soul, that immediately attracted his attention. It was she who told him that he ought to marry her, and so he did. Robby is the issue of that happy union.

Ames's letter to Robby is filled with family memories, poignant experiences, and theological insights. I'll focus on just a couple of these, avoiding altogether the main plot that is shared by the two novels. When he was a boy, Ames remembers the time that lightning struck the Baptist church and started a fire (*Gilead*, 95–96). The whole town turned out to salvage what they could. A warm rain began to fall, turning the ashes into watery soot. Ruined Bibles and hymnals were buried, and a prayer was said over them. Men and women worked together and sang softly, the women's hair falling behind their backs. Food was brought and shared. His father took an ash-covered biscuit, broke it, and gave it to him. Ames remembers this as an act of communion, and indeed it was—communion in the profoundest sense of receiving the body and blood of Christ, the body broken and the blood shed to share the pain and heal the community as it labored together.

Once, when the Lord's Supper was celebrated at his church, Ames preached on the words of institution (*Gilead*, 69–70).

Part 1: Summer Sermons

When he was finished with the service, his wife brought Robby up the aisle and said, "You ought to give him some of that." She was completely right. Ames began to appreciate the gifts of physical particularity and how blessing and sacrament are mediated through them—not simply human actions but images of nature, such as water and light (*Gilead*, 14, 23, 51, 119, 162, 246, etc.). He remembers being caught in rainstorms, playing in the river, seeing light flood the barren plains at sunrise and disappear suddenly at sunset. He remembers once seeing the full moon rise as the sun was setting, and thought of the whole earth as embraced by these two orbs. These are physical signs of an invisible grace—the hands of the Lord wrapped around the fragile passing world.

Water is not simply a sign of grace. It is also a powerful, destructive force. I am reminded of that in Nashville, my hometown, where terrible floods devastated parts of the city on May 1st and 2nd. But the response was the same as when the church burned in Gilead. Volunteers turned out in flooded neighborhoods, tearing out sodden drywall, removing ruined possessions, starting the slow process of recovery. Men and women worked side by side, neighbors brought food and drink, and acts of silent communion were shared.

Ames recalls many conversations with members of his congregation. A great part of his work had been listening to people, in the intense privacy of confession, or at least unburdening (*Gilead*, 44–45). These conversations were, he said, like a contest, or game, of which life is the real subject. By "life" he means not only energy and vitality but also the "incandescence" or "loveliness" in the presence shaped around the human "I" like "a flame on a wick, emanating itself in grief and guilt and joy and whatever else . . . quick, avid, and resourceful. To see this aspect of life is a privilege of the ministry which is seldom mentioned." Then Ames says that a good sermon is "one side of a passionate conversation." There are three parties to it, as there are even to the most private thought— "the self that yields the thought, the self that acknowledges and in some way responds to the thought, and the Lord."

Excursions into Difficulty

How is the Lord the party to a conversation? Since Ames does not elaborate, I offer my interpretation: the Lord is present *in* the conversation, *is* in a sense the conversation itself, the thought itself, the spiritual force that links the parties. In writing about the Trinity, St. Augustine draws analogies from love and knowledge: there is the lover, the beloved, and love itself; or the knower, the known, and knowledge itself; likewise there is the Father, the Son, and the Holy Spirit. The third term—love, knowledge, spirit—is the bond that links the other two. God is in fact all three terms, the lover and the beloved as well as love itself, and this means that God is an intrinsic relationality, the matrix that holds the world together, the creator of the communion that for human creatures is always a struggle and an adventure. Ames has learned to see this relationality in all that surrounds him, in nature as well as in the sheer, majestic fact of human existence.

A good sermon is one side of a passionate conversation. The role of the preacher is not principally to convey doctrine or teach morals, but to evoke a conversation, to raise questions and to seek answers with the congregation. The congregation becomes an active participant. African American and Pentecostal churches are notable in this regard. The action of call and response, when it gets going well, is a wondrous thing to behold. By "response" I don't mean simply emotions and bodily movements, though they have their place. I mean *thought*, and that's what Ames mentions in his illustration. The Lord is in the thought, the thinking process, that transpires when a group of people come together for celebration and reflection, reflection on the highest mysteries: a community at prayer and at thought. Thought requires words, and the words become sanctified, the visible sign of an invisible grace, the presence of the Lord in the midst of the people. Not only the water of baptism, not only the bread and wine of communion, but the words of this passionate conversation become sacraments. Ultimately everything can become a sacrament when we stop long enough to notice it and rejoice in it.

But wait a minute. What about the bad things, the terrible things, the accidents and illnesses, the greed and malice, the conflicts and tragedies? Water, wind, fire, words give life, but they also destroy. How does God's providence manifest itself when conversation and communion break down, and we are left with a broken heart? Is there no balm in Gilead, no healing for the wounds of God's people? This is the question that must give every sermon pause.

Marilynne Robinson notes the pause. In an interview, she comments on the idea that a good sermon is one side of a passionate conversation and then adds the following: "A sermon is a form that yields a certain kind of meaning in the same way that, say, a sonnet is a form that deals with a certain kind of meaning that has to do with putting things in relation to each other, allowing for the fact of complexity reversal, such things. Sermons are, at their best, *excursions into difficulty* that are addressed to people who come there in order to hear that."[2] I think this is a very profound insight. I wish that more ministers and congregations would be prepared to make such excursions, to dwell on difficult and complex matters, to engage in passionate conversations about them.

A prime example of such an excursion into difficulty is the sermon Ames once preached on the stories of Hagar and Ishmael and Abraham and Isaac found in Genesis, chapters 21–22 (*Gilead*, 129–30; *Home*, 206–7). Abraham's wife Sarah was too old to bear children. She had an Egyptian slave-girl whose name was Hagar. Sarah told Abraham to "go in to my slave-girl so that I might obtain children by her." Abraham did as he was told, and Hagar gave birth to a son, who was named Ishmael (we learn this several chapters earlier, in Genesis 16). But later (in Genesis 21) the Lord promised to give Sarah and Abraham a son of their own, despite their advanced years, and he was named Isaac. Sarah became jealous when she saw Ishmael and Isaac playing together. So she said to Abraham, "Cast out this slave woman with her son; for the son of this slave woman shall not inherit along with my son Isaac." Abraham was distressed, but the Lord approved of Sarah's demand, so again Abraham did as he was told. He gave Hagar bread and water and sent her away with the child into the wilderness of Beersheba.

2. Interview with *Religion & Ethics Newsweekly*. My italics.

When the provisions were used up, Ishmael would have died had not an angel of the Lord appeared to Hagar and showed her a well of water. Of Ishmael God said, "I will make a great nation."

In the next chapter of Genesis, God tested Abraham by telling him to take his son Isaac into the mountains and to offer him as a burnt offering. Once again, Abraham did as he was told, and he was about to sacrifice Isaac when the angel of the Lord intervened and provided a ram instead. These two stories have had fateful consequences in human history. The followers of Muhammad claim to be descendants of Ishmael, and the "great nation," they say, is the nation of Islam, born of the concubine, the Egyptian. Enmity between Arabs, Jews, and Christians has haunted many generations. The radically obedient faith of Abraham, his willingness to consign one son to the wilderness and to sacrifice the other, has been praised as the highest virtue and condemned as the most despicable crime. It drove Kierkegaard to write his book about faith called *Fear and Trembling*, and it has driven others to lose faith altogether.

Ames does not shy away from the difficulty of these stories, and he offers a novel interpretation of them. He describes his sermon to Robby: "My point was that Abraham is in effect called upon to sacrifice both his sons, and that the Lord in both instances sends angels to intervene at the critical moment to save the child. Abraham's extreme old age is an important element in both stories, not only because he can hardly hope for more children, not only because the children of old age are unspeakably precious, but also, I think, because any father, particularly an old father, must finally give his child up to the wilderness and trust to the providence of God. It seems also a cruelty for one generation to beget another when parents can secure so little for their children, so little safety, even in the best circumstances. Great faith is required to give the child up, trusting God to honor the parents' love for him by assuring that there will indeed be angels in that wilderness. I noted that Abraham himself had been sent into the wilderness, told to leave his father's house also, that this was the narrative of all generations, and that it is only by the grace of God that we are made instruments of his providence and participants in a fatherhood that is always ultimately his" (*Gilead*, 128–29).

"The narrative of all generations." This puts a different spin on the story. It's not simply about the terrible faith of Abraham but also about the human condition: generation follows upon generation, and each generation must at some point give up its children to the wilderness. Letting a child go is one of the hardest but inescapable decisions that parents have to make. We prepare our children as best we can, but then they go out into the world on their own, and we know what a savage world it can be, how little safety there is, what risks must be taken, what goals can be attained or lost, what compromises are inevitable. We don't stop bearing children, but we have to entrust our children to the providence of God. Abraham knows that, once Sarah has borne a legitimate son, his illegitimate son will have to leave the community. And he knows that God, having given him another son, can also take him away.

There is cruelty in these narratives. On this matter John Ames comments that children are often victims of rejection and violence. The Bible does not seem otherwise to countenance such cruelty, but even in these cases the child is within the providential care of God. "This [care] is no less true if the angel carries her home to her faithful and loving Father than if he opens the spring or stops the knife and lets the child live out her sum of earthly years." In both instances we speak of the providence of God. But, as Ames also emphasizes, we human beings are made instruments of God's providence and participants in the divine parenting. The stories attribute the working of this providence to the intervention of angels, but in fact it is *we* who are responsible. Our actions make a difference, even if we cannot prevent the hazards of the wilderness. Providence works by providing lures for our ideals and restraining the effects of our recalcitrant passions. We can avoid religious, cultural, and racial stereotyping, we can protect the weak and vulnerable, we can strengthen the fabric of the human community, we can overcome our selfishness and take seriously our responsibilities.

Excursions into Difficulty

Marilynne Robinson commented on the loss of seriousness in the interview to which I have referred. She says that in earlier times people actually wanted to make the world good for future generations that they would never see. Being serious about our responsibilities makes people think in very large terms to try to liberate women, for example, or to try to eliminate slavery (two of the great goals of the nineteenth century). Of course, she adds, slavery has come back all over the world now (child prostitution in Asia, involuntary servitude in Africa, even in the USA). People say, "Well, we won't think about that. It's too bad." Robinson is disturbed by the degree to which she doesn't hear them saying, "Are we leaving the world better than we found it?" She thinks we are a generation that perhaps could not answer in the affirmative; we evade the larger responsibility of being only one generation in what one hopes will be "an infinite series of fruitful generations." There is a selfishness in refusing to understand that we are simply "passing through."

It would help if ministers and theologians thought more about these ideas rather than simply emphasizing, for example, the finality of salvation in Christ. Salvation is in fact a long and difficult journey on which we human beings play a continuing role. Only eighty generations have passed since the time of Jesus, whereas there have been some two thousand generations since *Homo sapiens* first wandered out of Africa. Humankind faces a long road ahead if it does not render the world environmentally uninhabitable or destroy itself in nuclear warfare. Confronting difficulties at all levels, political as well as personal, is a major task of ministry, and in this regard much is to be learned from the imagination of Marilynne Robinson.

5

August 28, 2011

Wind[1]

Genesis 1:1-11, 2:4b-7; Psalm 104:1-4; John 3:1-10

You've heard the texts I have chosen, and you've traveled through wind and rain to get here today, so you probably know the topic of my sermon without its being printed in the bulletin. I could have tried to preach on the announced topic of "grace and work," but instead have chosen wind and spirit, a topic inspired by Hurricane Irene. I've looked at Mark Lyndaker-Studer's text, which is probably the lectionary text for the day, the parable of the talents, which culminates with these harsh words of Jesus: "For to all those who have, more will be given, and they will have an abundance; but from those who have nothing, even more will be taken away." These are strange words coming from the same Jesus who talked about setting all else aside to find the lost sheep. The talents are the reversal of the good shepherd or the good Samaritan. Perhaps the very strangeness, the reversal, is the point, the disruption of normal expectations occasioned by the

---

1. This sermon was prepared with about twenty-four hours' notice as a substitute for the announced pastor of the day, who could not reach Eagles Mere from Philadelphia because of flooded roads and high winds.

WIND

kingdom of God. I'll leave that text to Mark. I admire his courage in addressing it. It's a difficult text, even if you believe that grace precedes work.

At least I know something about wind and spirit, having written a book called *Winds of the Spirit* (1994). The word for "spirit" in Hebrew (*ruach*) means literally "wind," "moving air," "breath," or "breathing." The same is true of Greek (*pneuma*) and Latin (*spirare*). Spirit is like a wind. Wind is a material image of an immaterial vitality, a fluid, pervasive, intangible energy, whose fundamental purpose is to create, shape, enliven, and renew. As such it is a very powerful image of God, and the Hebrew Bible is filled with wind and spirit. God's wind swept over the face of the waters, shaping the world out of a formless void, and God breathed the breath of life into human beings. Breathing is essential to mammals, the inhaling and exhaling of air. Through little explosions and transmissions of air, human beings communicate by language. We couldn't talk in a vacuum, and without speech we wouldn't be human. Wind, air, breath: the essential stuff of life.

Spirit is associated with other basic elements in the Hebrew Bible: fire, light, water. They are connected by Psalm 104: "You are clothed with honor and mastery, wrapped in light as with a garment. You stretch out the heavens like a tent, you set the beams of your chambers on the waters, you make the clouds your chariot, you ride on the wings of the wind, you make the winds your messengers, fire and flame your ministers." Fire is produced by the rapid fusion of air (oxygen) with combustible substances, and it in turn produces heat and light. Spirit is a fusion that releases incredible energy. Water is closely related to air, a combination of hydrogen and oxygen (whereas air is a mixture mostly of nitrogen and oxygen). Water too is an image of God as spirit: "a fountain of living water" (Jeremiah 2:13), "a spring of water gushing up to eternal life" (John 4:14). Of course the ancients didn't know about the chemical composition of air and water, but they knew they were fluid, permeable, pervasive elements, essential to life, but also potentially destructive just because of their fluidity.

Part 1: Summer Sermons

"You ride on the wings of the wind": the wings of birds and the sails of ships. The seas were conquered by clever wooden devices, one of the most important of human inventions. Their sails have an aerodynamic function: a partial vacuum on the bulging side of the sail—a negative force—is what drives the ship (except when the wind is dead astern). Wind pushes but mostly pulls. The negative force is the key to flight (the airplane being another clever human invention, based on the same principle as sailing): "lift" is caused by a drop in air pressure on the upper side of the wing. Variations in air pressure cause wind in the first place, and these variations are extremely unpredictable on a small scale. "The wind blows where it chooses" (John 3:8).

This brings us to the Gospel of John and the story of Nicodemus, who is a Pharisee, a ruler and teacher of the Jews. He arrives by night (in secret) to find out whether Jesus has really come from God. He is so literal-minded that he can't comprehend what he is hearing. How can a person be "born anew" without entering the womb a second time? He has no sense of what it means to be born of water and the Spirit; or that such a second birth is necessary to enter the kingdom of God, which is a spiritual kingdom. Nicodemus fits into the negative stereotype that the author has of Jews, and he functions as a "fall guy" in the story, a means for getting the point across.

The point is important: a second birth is what connects us with the power of the Spirit. This is a tremendous power, the greatest of powers, but, like the wind itself, it can become extremely dangerous. God creates and controls this power. Jesus is the channel—or Moses, or Muhammad, or Buddha, or Brahman, or Socrates. We need as many channels as possible because humans can't be trusted with spiritual power. We need channels of the Spirit, sails to capture and direct its power. Think of Jesus as the sail on our ship of faith. Without him we would be dead in the water or blown every which way. He orients us by his wisdom and example. From him we learn that we cannot enter the kingdom of God without being born anew, without being born of the Spirit. But this Spirit, this wind, blows were it chooses; we may hear the sound of it, but we cannot see it and control it. We know not where it comes from or where it goes. In the case of Jesus, it leads to death before it brings new life. The way of the Spirit is the way of the cross.

Jesus' death—the discipline of the cross—reminds us to be wary of the fanaticism of spiritualist movements, from the ancient Montanists to present-day revivalists. Nazism was a fascist form of spirituality that offered the promise of rejuvenation for a defeated and demoralized nation. The Nazis created and lived *In the Garden of Beasts*—the title of a book by Erik Larson (2011), who describes Berlin in the mid-1930s and the family of the American ambassador who lived near the famous *Tiergarten* (animal park, with a zoo at one end). The greatest crimes of humanity are committed on behalf of demonic ideologies, by persons who are certain they are filled with the Spirit. The demonic is the nether side of the divine; spiritual possession is the destructive aspect of spiritual rebirth. How can these be so closely connected? We must learn to discern the spirits, and for Christians Jesus Christ is the discernment. The demons he cast out recognized him as their true adversary.

We give our hurricanes human names. We personify them. Why do we do this? We don't do for it any other destructive natural forces (tornadoes, forest fires, earthquakes, tsunamis). Is it because we are in certain respects like hurricanes, or they like us? We watch them as they form in the warm waters of the Gulf or the Atlantic, then follow with fascination and dread as they determine on a direction to blow and a speed with which to move. They seem to take on a personality of their own. This is something primordial about them, and about ourselves as well. We sense that we too participate in the awesome, creative/destructive power of life itself.

6

June 28, 2015

Your Faith Has Made You Well

Wisdom of Solomon 1:13–15; 2:23–24
Mark 5:21–43

Today is the beginning of summer for the Presbyterian Church of Eagles Mere. In terms of the astronomical calendar summer actually began a week ago, and at the end of this coming week we'll celebrate the Fourth of July, followed by the first Sports Week, so we're already almost into the thick of things in Eagles Mere. Summer goes by quickly here. In another six weeks the major activities will have ended and the young people will begin drifting away. So I thought a sermon on the beginning of a new season might be appropriate, or reflections on the nature of summer, or on the quick and relentless passage of time. There is grist in the mill of the Bible on the relentless passage of time, but not so much on the season of summer. Summer in the Bible is mostly the season in which crops grow and preparations are made for hard weather ahead. It is not, notably, a time of vacation. Psalm 32:4 does mention that "my strength was dried up as by the heat of summer," but this is David's reference to the fact that the hand of the Lord lies heavily on him, exhausting his strength. In Matthew and Mark, Jesus says that his disciples should learn a lesson from the fig tree: "as soon as its branch becomes tender and puts forth its leaves, you know that summer is near" (Mark 13:28). But this is intended by Jesus (according to the gospel writers) as a sign of the end of the age, along with the destruction of Jerusalem and the setting up of a desolating sacrilege. The sun will be darkened, the moon will not give its light, the stars will fall, and you will see the Son of Man coming in clouds with great power and glory. This is not a promising text for a sermon on the beginning of summer.

So rather than being seasonal I will be "lectional." The common lectionary for today offers an interesting selection of texts. One of them is from an apocryphal book, the Wisdom of Solomon, which is rarely mentioned from the pulpit.[1] I like this text because it contrasts so completely with the selection from the gospel, which in this case is Mark's version of the story about Jairus' daughter and the woman with a hemorrhage. The lectionary this year seems to be reading through Mark's gospel and pairs it with appropriate readings from the Old Testament. You probably have already heard a good many sermons on Mark.

But before we get to Mark, let's take a look at the Wisdom of Solomon. This book was composed in Greek by an unknown Hellenistic Jew, probably at Alexandria, in the latter part of the first century BC. It offers a lot of didactic exhortation, which purports to be the wisdom of Solomon. It really is quite philosophical, although it is written in a poetic parallelism characteristic of the Hebrew Bible. The theme for today is that "God did not make death," and "does not delight in the death of the living." Perhaps that should be the title of my sermon: God Did Not Make Death. Although the living do seem to die, their righteousness is really

---

1. The Apocrypha (meaning "things that are hidden") contains fifteen books that are included in the Greek version of the Old Testament (the Septuagint) but are not part of the Hebrew canon. Protestants have generally adhered to the Hebrew canon and have made little use of these books, but Catholics regard them as "deuterocanonical," that is, added later to the canon. These books were called "hidden" either because they contain esoteric ideas (positive sense) or because they should be kept out of sight (negative sense).

immortal. The author stresses this immortality in the first chapters of his book—an immortality that is to be understood as a gift from God, the gift of God's wisdom. God has made us in the image of his own eternity, and it is only through the "devil's envy" that death entered the world. By pretending to *be* God, and getting human beings to worship him rather than God, it is the devil who makes death. Does this mean that, if they had not fallen prey to the devil, human beings would actually be immortal, like God? This doesn't seem very plausible to me. It overlooks the realities of disease, suffering, and death that all living creatures experience. There is a sense in which God *does* make death if God makes creatures who are different from God, that is, mortal creatures. Death seems to be a condition of life that is not God's life, an unavoidable by-product, so to speak. So perhaps the author is saying that God provides ways for us to cope with this fact, by giving us wisdom in the midst of ignorance, and generosity in place of jealousy.

The Gospel story that is our main text for today, the story of the daughter of Jairus and the woman with the hemorrhage, is completely familiar with the realities of disease, suffering, and death. Here there is no talk about immortality, about God not making death, but about the struggles of daily life. I've read Mark's version of this story (ch. 5), which, uncharacteristically in this instance, is more fully developed than the parallel versions of the story in Matthew (ch. 9) and Luke (ch. 8).[2] Mark leaves out a great deal that is found in Matthew and Luke—such as the annunciation and birth stories, many of Jesus' sayings and teachings (e.g., the Sermon on the Mount), and even the resurrection. Mark is a bare-bones gospel, but he does seem to relish stories about Jesus' healings and other miracles, which serve as proof that Jesus is what Mark says he is in the very first verse, the Son of God (Mark 1:1). But strangely, in Mark no one seems to recognize this except the demons, and Jesus orders witnesses not to tell anyone what has

---

2. Matthew, Mark, and Luke are called the "Synoptic" Gospels because they have a lot of parallel passages. Which is the earliest text, and who copied from whom, or whether there was a now-lost "sayings source," are issues that have been debated for two hundred years. John is a completely different Gospel with its own distinctive agenda.

happened. In any event, Mark is a good storyteller, and our text for today is a good example of his skill.

Jairus is one of the rulers of the synagogue. His little daughter is near death, and he begs Jesus to come and lay hands on her. A crowd gathers, and in the crowd is a woman who has suffered from hemorrhages for twelve years. No physician has been able to cure her. She interrupts the story about Jairus' daughter by coming up to Jesus and saying, "If I but touch his clothes, I will be well." She does touch him, and her flow of blood ceases. But Jesus is immediately aware that "power has gone forth from him" and asks who touched him. The woman confesses, "in fear and trembling," that it was she. Jesus says to her, "Daughter, your faith has made you well; go in peace, and be healed of your disease." In the meantime, people have come from Jairus' house reporting that his daughter has died already and there is no need to trouble the Teacher any further. But Jesus says to him, "Do not fear, only believe." He goes to the house and finds the child motionless. He says not to worry; she is not dead but only sleeping. To the disbelief of the bystanders he takes the child by hand and says to her, "Little girl, get up!" She does so immediately and walks about, for she is twelve years old (her age being one of the little details found only in Mark[3]). The witnesses were overcome by amazement, but Jesus "strictly ordered them that no one should know this, and told them to give her something to eat." (Concern about feeding the girl is also found only in Mark. Matthew's version ends the opposite way: the report of this healing "went through all that district.")

Even rulers of the synagogue are powerless when it comes to physical illness, and word has gotten about that Jesus can be of help in such cases. Before he can go to Jairus' house, however, he is interrupted by the woman with the hemorrhage. She believes that if she can touch even the fringe of his garment, she will be made well. Just the barest touch is sufficient (according to Matthew and

---

3. Is there any significance to the number twelve? The woman also suffered her hemorrhage for twelve years. There are after all twelve disciples, representing the twelve tribes of Israel. Perhaps the woman and the girl are types of Israel.

Luke), but Jesus is immediately aware that power has gone forth from him. When the woman confesses her touch with "fear and trembling," she is like Abraham as he prepared to sacrifice his son Isaac, his faith being tested to the limit by the Lord. (Kierkegaard wrote a book about this called *Fear and Trembling*.) But Jesus says to her, "Daughter, your faith has made you well; go in peace, and be healed of your disease." The power that went forth from Jesus must have been the power not of magic but of faith. Faith itself is a gift of God, but it must be internalized and activated by the believer. It is an activity, a conviction, a way of conducting oneself. It is a mentality that can actually help to cure the body. People have known this for the ages, so this story resonates with them. Today we know much more about the mind-body connection, and how the mind can release healing powers into the body through chemistry. This story is not interested in chemistry, in how the healing occurs, but simply in the fact that faith does have this power, and that such faith is a co-product, so to speak, of God and human beings. God gives faith, just as God gives the ram that was sacrificed in place of Isaac, but faith is also a human responsibility, something we do for ourselves and others. It requires the merest touch—touching the Lord and touching one's fellow human beings. The touch signifies that corporality is important, that human beings are embodied creatures who get sick, suffer, and die, that God somehow takes on this human form, suffers with us, and dies. Your faith has made you well. But when your time comes, you will die. That will be all right because God too has undergone death and will raise us to new life, the ongoing life of the faith-community. God does not deny death; rather God's gift of life triumphs over it. In this sense we can say, with the Wisdom of Solomon, that God did not make death and does not delight in the death of the living.

The themes of fear and faith reappear in the last part of our story. When people come from the house of Jairus to say that his daughter has died already and that he should no longer bother the Teacher, Jesus responds, "Do not fear, only believe." Jesus takes the motionless girl by the hand (physical touch again) and says two words to her in Aramaic: "Talitha cum," which means "Little girl, get up!" (Mark is the only gospel that gives the words in Aramaic, another touch of realism.) Jesus is addressed as "the Teacher," and it is his *words*, his *teachings*, that heal the human condition, because he talks about faith, love, hope, and the coming kingdom of God in which all God's creatures are taken up into God's presence. The kingdom of God happens when the faith of a woman puts an end to her hemorrhage and a word to a little girl restores her life. This is what the kingdom is like. It does not come with supernatural signs or apocalyptic violence, but simply is in our midst.

But there is one more point. Jesus strictly charges the witnesses that they should tell no one what has happened. Some scholars say this is evidence of Mark's "messianic secret." Mark tells his readers at the beginning who Jesus is, but the followers of Jesus discover his identity only gradually. Apparently Jesus did not go around bragging that he was the Son of God or the Messiah of Israel. Rather the focus is on his deeds and his words, and on the faith of his followers. When he tells them directly who he is, if he ever does, they already inwardly know it. Jesus contradicts all the standard messianic expectations. He does not come as a King who rescues the Jews from Roman domination. Rather he dies on a cross. But strangely, this powerless ending is full of amazing power. It is the power of faith, of a mustard seed, a tiny thing that grows into a great bush. Your faith has made you well. It means that God shares our mortality and overcomes it, because God does not make death as an end in itself and does not delight in the death of the living.

7

May 27, 2016

Audacity and Humility

Memorial Service for the Class of 1956, Sixtieth Reunion
Princeton University Chapel

First, I want to thank Sue Rodgers for planning this memorial service. For her it was a labor of love because five years ago she and her late husband, Bob, planned the service for our fifty-fifth reunion. Bob was a class leader active in many reunion activities, recipient of an Alumni Service Award, and he is sorely missed. So for Sue this is a poignant moment, as it is for me because five years ago Coleman Brown stood in this place, sharing with us thoughts about life and death, reflecting on a poem by Dylan Thomas, "And Death Shall Have No Dominion." Coleman *stood* here, straight and unassisted, even though by that stage of life he was confined to a wheelchair. Coleman was class president for three of our four years at Princeton. He was a bold leader, brought important issues to our attention, and took steps to insure that each and every class member received a bid from an eating club. I and many others benefited from his efforts, and he became for me a kind of hero. I admired him for helping to move Princeton toward a more equitable system, which began to materialize twenty years later with the establishment of residential colleges. Following graduation, Coleman went to Union Theological Seminary where he earned divinity and doctoral degrees. He returned to his hometown of Chicago and worked for a number of years in an inner-city parish. Then he accepted a call to Colgate as University Chaplain and Professor of Religion, where he had a profound influence on a generation of students.

Coleman died in December 2014, so he is among those being memorialized today. During the decade prior to his death, I visited him several times and learned the meaning of courage in the face of adversity. He suffered several strokes, which incapacitated his body, but he was always cheerful and never complained: he made the best of what was left to him, and he always wanted to talk about important matters. A year after his death, in December 2015, Irene, his wife of fifty-eight years, sent out a holiday card. On the front is a photo of Irene with her grandchildren, one of whom is graduating from Princeton next week. On the inside is a photo from 1994 of Coleman standing next to a blackboard, on which he has written the words "Audacity and Humility," followed by a question, "How to hold them together?" How typically Coleman! I thought. Challenging his students to discuss a difficult question. Forcing them to face the moral complexities of life.

Audacity and Humility. I decided to check these words in a biblical concordance. It comes as no surprise that audacity is not a Jewish or Christian virtue. It is found only once in the whole of scripture, in 3 Maccabees, a book of the Apocrypha, which is concerned with the struggle of Egyptian Jews who suffered under Ptolemy IV in the second century BC. Ptolemy is described as "an impious and profane man, puffed up in his audacity and power." Here "audacity" is used in a negative sense, meaning "arrogance" and "insolence." There is also a positive sense, meaning "boldness," "courage," "daring." Think of the great heroes of the Hebrew Bible: Abraham, Moses, David—surely they were audacious in both senses! Abraham, the great patriarch of Israel, who was prepared to sacrifice his second son Isaac in a test of faith, and who abandoned

Part 1: Summer Sermons

his first son, Ishmael, in the wilderness. Moses, who led his people out of Egypt but died before he could reach the promised land. Moses, who dared to climb up the holy mountain and bring down stone tablets containing God's commandments—who tried to see God face to face, but to whom God turned his backside. And then there was David, who as a young man killed Goliath with a slingshot, but who as king of Israel seduced Bathsheba, sent her husband to death in battle, then married the widow and had a child by her. Nathan prophesied that the child would die because "the thing that David had done displeased the Lord." When the child was dead, David said, "I will go to him, but he will not return to me." Audacity and humility. This is the same David who wrote some of the most beautiful Psalms, including the Twenty-Third.[1]

For Christians the greatest exemplar of humility is undoubtedly Jesus of Nazareth. We have heard what is written in the Epistle to the Philippians (2:3–7): "Do nothing from selfish ambition or conceit, but in humility regard others as better than yourselves. Let each of you look not to your own interests, but to the interests of others. Let the same mind be in you that was in Christ Jesus, who, though he was in the form of God, did not regard equality with God as something to be exploited, but emptied himself, taking the form of a servant." Yet this is the same Jesus who boldly proclaimed the coming of God's kingdom, contradicted the established interpretation of the law, performed healings on the Sabbath, transformed the concept of the Messiah, and sent out disciples to the ends of the earth. Nothing could be more audacious than that! He taught the paradox that one finds one's life by losing it, and he himself was obedient to the point of death (Matt 10:39; Phil 2:8).

Today we are memorializing eighty-one classmates who died between 2011 and the end of 2015. I've looked at what they wrote about themselves in our Fiftieth Reunion Book. Many of them went into business or finance, and some founded their own businesses (to me, an audacious step). The professions of law, medicine, science, and engineering were well represented. A fewer number became teachers and scholars, and a very few chose ministry. In

---

1. Sung at our memorial service by the Tigertones.

this group we also find an apple grower, a linguist, a foreign service officer, an antique wooden boat hobbyist, and several amateur poets. Some of these men were active in class leadership, others mentioned service projects, and many gave generously to good causes. Typical of Princeton classes in the 1950s, they—and we—were homogeneous, male, and privileged. Today Princeton has changed quite radically, and we can only rejoice in the diversity that now prevails.

These eighty-one classmates join those who have gone before them, so now we have lost 277, nearly half our entire class. Signs of our mortality are present. In another ten years, many if not most of us who are here today will be gone; and in another twenty years, the class of 1956 will be but a memory. We are in the twilight of our mortal existence, and the sense of approaching death is a great equalizer. Our proud achievements are laid low in the presence of a common denominator. Most of us do not complain, knowing that we have had more than our fair share of life, and we are grateful for what we have accomplished and what has been given us. We know that, to have made something of our lives, we needed audacity, but to temper that audacity, to prevent it from becoming puffed up, we also needed humility. Humility includes recognizing that death is not only inescapable but necessary. If humans, animals, and plants lived indefinitely, the earth would soon be choked by its own fecundity, and life on the planet would come to an end. We must die so that life can go on—the great chain of life in which we have had our small but significant place. With this recognition, death need have no dominion over us.

8

AUGUST 14, 2016

Hearing

Isaiah 6:8–11; Matthew 13:10–17

Our topic today is "hearing." Hearing is on my mind because last spring I acquired new hearing aids. My previous hearing aids dated from 2002 and still functioned well, but I didn't like to wear them. I enjoyed the world of relative silence that engulfed me, cutting me off from the outside world to some degree. My wife complained that she had to shout at me and said we were not communicating well. So I agreed to go to the audiology clinic, and I promised I would wear the new hearing aids more regularly than the old ones.

The new hearing aids are super, and super-complicated. They come with a uDirect 3 device and a uTV 3 device, and three instruction books with many pages each. I'm wearing the uDirect 3 around my neck. Its purpose is to stream audio from Bluetooth and other audio devices, and, in conjunction with the uTV 3, sound from a TV. It can also be used to change audio programs and adjust the sound level. The only part of the technology I've mastered is the TV part. The uTV 3 plugs into the audio-out jack of the TV, and, when paired with the uDirect 3, puts the TV sound

HEARING

directly into my ears. All sorts of annoying sounds now become audible, and I can really hear almost too well.

Most people don't realize how important hearing is to the Bible. When you look at a complete concordance, you find there are 1,278 occurrences of "hear" and its cognates ("heard," "hearer," "hearing," etc.). This is even more than the 1,014 occurrences of "see" and its cognates. Then when you add the 2,928 occurrences of "say" and its cognates, and the 670 occurrences of "speak" and its cognates, you realize that speaking and hearing are absolutely fundamental to biblical religion. Of course the Bible is the product of a highly oral culture, and orality, not writing, is the principal means of communication. Ironically, today with all our phones, we mostly text, not talk. But speaking and hearing are the means by which God communicates with us. No one has seen God (God turned his face away from Moses), but we certainly hear God speaking, out of the thunder of the holy mountain, or through the commandments of the law, or by the mouths of prophets, and even babes and infants.

Most of the occurrences of "hearing" and "saying" in the Bible are quite unexceptional, just ordinary discourse. But a theological motif echoes in the background of both Testaments: people hear *but do not really hear*, they listen *but do not comprehend*, "their ears are hard of hearing." Likewise they see but do not really see, they look but do not understand. Isaiah is told by the Lord that, because of the people's obtuseness, his mission is to "stop their ears and shut their eyes." When Isaiah asks, "how long, O Lord?" he is told, "Until cities lie waste without inhabitant, and houses without people, and the land is utterly desolate." Without hearing the word of God, people are cut off from life.

Jesus picks up this motif from Isaiah when he explains to the disciples why he speaks in parables. To the disciples it has been given to know "the secrets of the kingdom of heaven," but to the people it has not been given. The core is the verse that is found in all three of the Synoptic Gospels, and probably goes back to Jesus himself, quoting Isaiah: "The reason I speak to them in parables is that 'seeing they do not perceive, and hearing they do not listen, nor do they understand.' " Only Matthew adds the full quotation from Isaiah. John leaves out hearing and seeing, and converts the point into the importance of believing, of having faith.

What is going on here? What is it we do not see when we look, and do not understand when we hear? Could I see it if I put on glasses, or hear it if I wore hearing aids? We get the impression that these devices won't help, that it is not a matter of physical blindness or deafness, but rather a matter of a spiritual blindness and deafness. But what is this spiritual thing that I cannot see or hear, and why is faith required to comprehend it?

The question from the disciples about why Jesus spoke in parables was prompted by his telling a parable, the one about a sower and his seed, which is found just prior to the passage I read from Matthew. The parable is so simple as to seem almost banal. The seeds that fell on the path are eaten up by birds. The seeds that fell on rocky ground produced weak sprouts that dried out and withered away. The seeds that fell among thorns were choked out by the thorns. But "other seeds fell on good soil and brought forth grain, some a hundredfold, some sixty, some thirty. Let anyone with ears listen!"

OK, we are listening, but what are we supposed to hear and comprehend? What is it that we are deaf to? The seeds themselves must be fertile, so it depends entirely on the kind of soil they fall on as to whether they bring forth grain. *We* must be the soil, and our hearing and seeing, or deafness and blindness, must be what makes the soil good or bad. Is this the secret of the kingdom of God? It seems to be, in part. The thing we cannot hear and see is God, the presence of God, the reign and realm of God. Yet without our hearing and seeing, there is no kingdom, no presence, no God. God is there when faith is active in love; without faith, God is absent. We are part of the connection by which God is efficacious in the world. In case there is any doubt about the meaning, Jesus goes on to explain the parable in the passage following the one I read. He says: if we hear the word of the kingdom and do not understand it, the evil one snatches away what is sown in the heart, just as the seeds on the path are eaten by birds. As for what is sown on rocky ground, this is the person who hears the word superficially and forgets it when trouble arises. As for what is sown among thorns, this is the person who hears the word, but the cares of the world and the lure of wealth choke the word, and it yields nothing. But as for what was sown on good soil, this is the person who hears the word and understands it.

Doesn't this put a terrible responsibility on us? Yes, it does. Perhaps that is why Isaiah says that, when people stop their ears and shut their eyes, cities lie waste, houses are without inhabitants, and the land is utterly desolate and empty. For the most part, we live in a wasteland, a land without meaning and purpose, a land where instant gratifications provide the only relief. We seek escape rather than doing the hard work of making the kingdom of God actual in our midst. This hard work requires a constant attending to the Spirit of God. Sounds of the Spirit are not something my uDirect 3 can pick up.

Of course, it is not just our responsibility. The seed is *given* to us, is sown right onto and into us, and the seed is the word of God. We don't produce or imagine God. The reality of God presents itself to us, but it is the hardest and most difficult thing to detect. This reality is in our hearts, in our inner seeing and hearing. If we hear and comprehend it from within, it has the most amazing and transforming power, bringing forth a hundredfold, an enormous yield. "To those who have, more will be given, and they will have an abundance; but from those who have nothing, even what they have will be taken away."

Jesus hints at what happens when God is present. The poor have good news brought to them; captives are released and the oppressed go free; the blind recover their sight and the deaf their hearing. Human beings flourish; they go out in the world to contribute what they can, and they gather together in celebration and worship. The signs of the kingdom are practical, a matter of how we live more than how we think (but thought is important!). A tremendous power is released, far exceeding our expectations. God is roaring all around us. Do you not hear?

9

SEPTEMBER 3, 2017

Feet

Psalm 31:1–8; Matthew 28:1–10

"You have set my feet in a broad place" (Psalm 31:8)

Feet are a neglected part of our bodies. We normally don't think about them or look at them very much. They aren't beautiful and become ugly as they age. But we walk on them every day.

I didn't think about my feet until a problem occurred last summer—a sharp pain in my right heel as I was playing tennis. I hoped the pain would go away in a few days, and I continued to play tennis. The pain persisted and I went to the Laporte Medical Clinic, where an osteopathic doctor affixed a name to my problem: plantar fasciitis. Not much to be done about it, he said; give it a rest for a few weeks and take Naproxen. I didn't follow his advice and injured the heel again later in the summer. I looked up "plantar fasciitis" and discovered that the problem is not in the heel itself but in the ligaments (the plantar fascia) that connect the heel to the toes. These ligaments can become inflamed and cause spurs to form at the front of the heel bone. I learned that the foot is an incredibly complex mechanism, capable of being maneuvered in all directions, and of bearing the weight of our bodies over a lifetime. Beautiful in function if not in form. When I returned to Nashville I saw an orthopedist who said the same thing for a much higher fee and gave me exercises. I bought a bicycle, stayed off my feet for a couple of months, and finally the healing began.

You would be amazed at how frequently the words "feet" and "foot" appear in the Bible (264 occurrences of "feet," 114 of "foot"). People were just more conscious of feet in those days. They were the chief means of transportation and well taken care of. Roads were dusty, foot-washings were common, and feet achieved a kind of venerated status. People walked thousands of miles during a lifetime, whereas today we generally walk as little as possible. Eventually our feet may atrophy.

Last November a close friend of mine in Germany passed away. Call him George. We had been roommates at Yale Divinity School in the fall of 1958. It was just at that time that I had begun seeing a young woman named Eva. I told George that he should have a date for a big football weekend when Eva and her roommate, and my former college roommate, would all be present. George went to the Yale Graduate School and asked for a list of female German graduate students. He actually interviewed a few of them and finally settled on Sybille, who had just started a doctoral program in Slavic languages. After that weekend, George and Sybille began seeing each other every day. To the astonishment of everyone, they were married six weeks later in Dwight Chapel at Yale!

George had an amazing life. In the winter of 1944, when he was fourteen years old, he was drafted into the German army and told to defend the Fatherland. I don't think he ever fired a shot. At some point he was taken to Austria where he stayed until the end of the war. He didn't like to talk about this part of his life. He began university studies, and in 1952 received a World Council of Churches scholarship to study at the Oberlin School of Theology. Then he enrolled in a doctoral program at Yale. After he and Sybille were married, he taught at a college in Illinois for a few years, until

Part 1: Summer Sermons

they returned to Germany with two small daughters. After a parish assignment and a stint in Berlin, he became a professor of ethics at a Lutheran theological seminary in Neuendettelsau, a small town near Nuremberg. In his last years he suffered a debilitating stroke, which paralyzed him until his death. We last visited George and Sybille in 2012 about a year before the stroke. George left behind an unpublished autobiography and instructions for his funeral. He chose a passage from Psalm 31 as the text: "You have set my feet in a broad place." George loved the Psalms, and he knew them very well. A former colleague who spoke at the service developed the theme of Psalm 31:8 as it applied to George's life. His feet had indeed been set in a broad place—from the ruins of Nazi Germany to study in America to the good fortune of having me as a roommate to various pastorates and teaching positions until he ended up at the Augustana Hochschule. His fairly strict Lutheranism was challenged at Yale, and his fairly rigorous personality softened and opened up as the years went on. He became a popular teacher because he liked to engage his students in discussion and debate, a novelty for German students who mostly listened to lectures. His path was further broadened when he spent time in Israel and Palestine, and, with Sybille, in Tanzania. George assumed that the "broad place" meant that human beings are given the freedom to choose their own course in life, to follow their own direction. Some people would say that what we do with the broad place is a matter of chance or fate or luck. But according to the psalmist, it is *the Lord* who has set our feet in a broad place. George believed that too, but sometimes he doubted it. Haven't we all?

The preacher at George's service pointed out that the broad place doesn't necessarily mean the high place, the High Noon of our lives. In the verses immediately following our text the psalmist writes (vss. 9–10):

> Be gracious to me, O Lord, for I am in distress;
> my eye wastes away from grief,
> my soul and body also.
> For my life is spent with sorrow, and my years with sighing;

> my strength fails because of my misery,
> and my bones waste away.

So the broad place includes the low places and the dead ends, including the final resting place. George and Sybille's oldest daughter died of leukemia. George spent his last two and a half years in a wheelchair, his feet no longer touching the ground. But even then, if we believe the psalmist, the Lord has seen our afflictions, and his steadfast love continues. It is into his hand that we commit our spirit. We are given broad places, but we are drawn back to the One Place at the end.

I read a passage from the Gospel of Matthew, which tells how the women went to the tomb of Jesus and found an angel sitting on a stone, who told them that Jesus was not there because he had been raised from the dead and gone ahead of them to Galilee. Jesus was on his feet again. Suddenly he met them on the road to Galilee. Matthew says, "they came to him, took hold of his feet, and worshiped him." They took hold of his feet. What a strange idea! Holding feet must have been a form of salutation and veneration. When the Shunammite woman came to Elisha on the mountain, "she caught hold of his feet"; and when Elisha told her that her child was alive (having sneezed seven times), "she came and fell at his feet" (2 Kgs 4:27, 37). So feet were important to human relations and respect. Here, take my feet, not my hands. My *feet* have been set in a broad place. Jesus suggests as much when he says to the women, "Do not be afraid; go and tell my brothers to go to Galilee; there they will see me." Jesus' raising means that his broad place has become a universal place. His sisters and brothers have a commission to spread the good news, to make disciples of all nations, to minister to the poor and suffering, to set captives free, to welcome refugees, to ensure that people are healthy and educated. We too are called to stand on our feet and get to work.

Well, I can't stop quite yet. I haven't said enough for a proper sermon. I need another couple of minutes. So I'll meditate a little further on the feet of the resurrected Jesus. The important thing about the resurrection story, in my view, is not that a physical miracle has transpired, that a dead body has literally come back to life. That would take us off the hook and leave us with nothing to do. The Gospel of Matthew does seem to emphasize the physical aspect. Luke and John place more emphasis on the spiritual appearances of Jesus to the disciples, and on the fact that they recognize him only when he speaks to them. But with Matthew physicality is important. It is Jesus' *feet* that were pierced (as well as other parts of his body), and the disciples recognize him when they take hold of his feet. But when you think about it, you realize that *we* have become the feet of Jesus, and that our collective feet have made his broad place a universal place. In the resurrection a *transition* occurs from Jesus to the Holy Spirit and the community of faith. When Jesus departs the Spirit is sent (John, ch. 14). This Spirit needs feet to do God's work in the world. Tomorrow is Labor Day, so let's get on our feet and go to work.

An African tradition says that we take two steps forward and one step back. We followed that tradition during my fiftieth reunion at Yale Divinity School, as we marched out of the chapel singing the South African hymn "Siyahamba—We Are Marching in the Light of God." Life is a long march with many setbacks. But eventually you get to the destination.

"Siyahamba" is not in our hymnal, but "Kum ba Yah" is (no. 338). We'll sing it as our closing hymn. I've added two verses: "Someone's marching Lord, kum ba yah; Someone's walking Lord, kum ba yah." It's printed in the bulletin. You are welcome to remain in your seats, but I invite you to get into the aisle and march out, taking two steps forward and one step back.

10

JULY 22, 2018

Abba

Mark 14:35–36, Romans 8:15–17, Galatians 4:6

"Abba, for you all things are possible" (Mark 14:36).

Bob Linders, of St. Paul's Lutheran Church in Doylestown, preaches every summer to us Presbyterians here in Eagles Mere. He's a remarkable preacher and a remarkable person. He has served as senior pastor at St. Paul's since 1977, and before that he was the New Jersey state champion in the eight-hundred-meter run in 1960. Obviously he is in for the long run at St. Paul's. He has lectured or preached at Princeton, Cornell, and Penn State, and has published several collections of sermons. I mention all this because a couple of years ago Bob told us about a book he was reading and finding helpful, a book by John Cobb called *Jesus' Abba: The God Who Has Not Failed*. When Bob says something like that, I pay attention, so I bought the book and read it.

John Cobb was ninety years old when this book was published in 2015. He has written many books and is one of my favorite theologians. He has made use of what is called "process philosophy"

Part 1: Summer Sermons

to rethink the idea of God and to develop a new interpretation of the Christian faith. His views are beautifully summed up in *Jesus' Abba*, and he has written the book very simply so it is accessible to laypeople, except perhaps for a few sections.

Cobb proposes to think about God as Jesus did.[1] It is highly probable that Jesus spoke Aramaic. He thought of God as *Abba*, which is the Aramaic word for "father." In the Bible there are two major images of God, monarchical and familial, God as "King" and God as "Father." Divine sovereignty came to dominate Christian thought, but Jesus himself spoke only of God as his and our Father. Confusion occurs because Jesus' central message was that the "kingdom of God" is at hand and that people must repent to enter it. It is natural to move from the idea of a kingdom to the idea that we should image God as king. But the Greek word translated as "kingdom" is *basileia*. A *basileia* is a politically defined region. If God is like a father, then his region or land will not be a kingdom but a family estate. This estate would be managed for the sake of all who live there with a special concern for the weak and needy. The best word for this, says Cobb, might be "commonwealth," a community arranged for the well-being of all. Ann Patchett in her novel *Commonwealth* (2016) describes a community formed of a blended family brought about by a divorce and remarriage. The two sisters from one set of parents are thrown together with the two brothers and two sisters of the other set of parents during summers in Virginia, where they create a kind of messy commonwealth. Tragedy occurs in this commonwealth (as it does in God's commonwealth) with the death of the older boy from a bee sting. And the community is formed as the result of a failure in human relations. God does not directly control this commonwealth, but God is nonetheless present, in the background as it were, as a spiritual presence and guide, promoting the well-being of all.[2]

1. Cobb, *Jesus' Abba*, materials from the preface and chaps. 1 and 3.

2. Another version of a family commonwealth is found in the Canadian TV series *Heartland*. Several generations of an extended family live together on a horse ranch, presided over by the patriarch, Jack. The central figure is his granddaughter, Amy, the "miracle girl," who heals not only horses but humans (with a combination of empathy, sensitivity, and intelligence). Conflicts,

Cobb says that the idea of God's omnipotence is not in the Bible, although most people seem to think of God all-powerful. Cobb believes, and I agree, that the whole idea of divine omnipotence is self-destructive—that is, the explanation that God can control whatever he wishes, but gives some power to us humans to obey or disobey. If God is omnipotent, it is amazing that God does not wish to end some of the horrors of history or the extreme suffering of individuals! It's hard to combine God's permitting so much misery with the idea of his paternal love. But by the end of the fourth century of the Christian era, the monarchical view came to dominate reflection about God. This is partly because St. Jerome used the Latin word *omnipotens* ("Almighty") to translate one of the Hebrew names for God, *Shaddai* (which has more the meaning of "presence"). Theologians developed elaborate theories about God's omnipotence, omniscience, and omnipresence.

Of course "Abba" is baby talk, like "papa" and "mamma." But Cobb points out that it was the only term in Aramaic for "father." Jesus thought of God in a language whose earliest and primary connotation came from infancy. The normal relation of a father to an infant is one of tenderness and unconditional love rather than controlling power. Cobb argues that the occurrences of *Abba* in the New Testament are not baby talk but something quite different. Jesus prayed to God in anguish in Gethsemane. According to the Gospel of Mark, "he threw himself on the ground and prayed that, if it were possible, the hour might pass from him. He said, 'Abba, Father, for you all things are possible; remove this cup from me; yet, not what I want, but what you want'" (Mark 14:35–36). So the only actual occurrence of "Abba" in the Gospels is associated with the passion of Jesus and his need for assistance. The other Gospels simply use the Greek word *pater*, "Father," when Jesus speaks of God.

---

adventures, and tragedies occur among the family, but also reconciliations and solutions—with Amy often at the center. This family estate promotes the well-being of all who live there and their friends. While not at all religious in intent, *Heartland*—the land of the heart—seems to offer an earthly image of the *basileia*.

Part 1: Summer Sermons

But it's interesting that the word "Abba" comes up again in two passages in the Apostle Paul where he is talking about the children of God being led by the Spirit of God. In Romans, chapter 8 (vss. 15–17), he writes: "For you did not receive a spirit of slavery to fall back into fear, but you have received a spirit of adoption. When we cry, 'Abba! Father!' it is that very Spirit bearing witness with our spirit that we are children of God, and if children, then heirs, heirs of God and joint heirs with Christ—if, in fact, we suffer with him so that we may also be glorified with him." And in Galatians, chap. 4 (vs. 6), he says: "And because you are children, God has sent the Spirit of his Son into our hearts, crying, 'Abba! Father!' So you are no longer a slave but a child, and if a child then also an heir, through God." So when we cry, "Abba," it is God's Spirit bearing witness with our spirit that we are children of God, and as children not slaves but inheritors of God's glory, "the freedom of the glory of the children of God" (Romans 8:21). Abba is the one who gives freedom and is the liberator from sin, law, and death.

All of this leads into the view that God's activity does not exclude other actors, so that the total explanation of an event includes both God and others. Various spiritual forces are in play. God works in and through natural things and especially human beings, bringing order out of chaos, striving for justice, freedom, and love. God's role is not control as such but "pushing" or "pulling" in a particular direction. In one of his earliest books, Cobb described God as our "companion," as one who is always with us in the here and now, and as one "who calls us forward" into new and more creative possibilities for our lives. God is something like a receptacle of possibilities, and God offers us the best possibility in every situation, but whether we choose that possibility or another course of action is up to us. The God who calls us forward is the source of novelty and freedom in our lives. Such a view is confirmed by the philosophy of Whitehead, and in the natural world it is hinted at by quantum physics. But this is getting too philosophical, and I won't go further in this direction, except to say that some people call what we are talking about here "chance," whereas we call it "God." Calling it God signifies that there is meaning, direction, and purpose in the world. Chance and randomness certainly play a central role in the evolutionary and historical process, but they can become instruments of divine purpose.

I've been preaching a sermon looking for texts, whereas the proper way of going about things is to start with texts looking for a sermon. But having gone this far, I can't turn back. One immediate objection to speaking of God as "Abba" is that it is masculine, gendered language. But the attributes associated with "Abba" seem to be feminine just as much if not more so than masculine. Cobb says that Jesus might have spoken of God not as his father but as his mother. Mary seems to have played a much larger role in his life than Joseph, and a much larger role among his followers. In some forms of Catholicism, she plays a larger role than even Jesus himself. So was it not maternal characteristics more than paternal ones that shaped Jesus' understanding of God? If that question had arisen in Jesus' day, he would have agreed, says Cobb. But it was not possible in Jesus' day to call God "Mother," because that would have made people think that he was calling them to worship a female deity alongside the God of Abraham, Isaac, and Jacob.

In recent times we have experimented with nongendered language for God. Patriarchy certainly has been destructive, and God is certainly not a male or a female. But a neutered God feels less intimate and supports abstract rather than familial language. When it comes to personal relationships, we are stuck with male and female, masculine and feminine, or some combination of them. Matriarchy is not a substitute for patriarchy, but there are feminine metaphors for God in the Bible, even though in a minor key.

One example is found in the sixty-sixth chapter of Isaiah, where the prophet imagines God as Mother Jerusalem: "Rejoice with Jerusalem, and be glad for her, all you who love her; rejoice with her in joy, all who mourn over her—that you may nurse and be satisfied from her consoling breast; that you may drink deeply with delight from her glorious bosom. . . . As a mother comforts her child, so I will comfort you; you shall be comforted in Jerusalem" (vss. 10–13).

Part 1: Summer Sermons

The Jerusalem imagery is used quite differently by Jesus in the twenty-third chapter of Matthew: "Jerusalem, Jerusalem, the city that kills the prophets and stones those who are sent to it! How often have I desired to gather your children together as a hen gathers her brood under her wings, and you were not willing!" (vss. 37–38). Now it is not Jerusalem that comforts but a lowly hen, who gathers her brood under her wings. This is the closest that Jesus comes to speaking of God as a mother.

Finally, following the Lukan version of the Beatitudes in chapter 6, Jesus talks about love (vss. 32–38). It's not good enough to love those who love you, for even sinners do that. Or lend to those from whom you hope to receive. "But love your enemies, do good, and lend, expecting nothing in return." Then you will be "children of the Most High, for he is kind to the ungrateful and the wicked. Be merciful, just as your Father is merciful." In the abstract sense, God is love—pure, unrequited, generous and self-giving love. In the concrete sense, the Most High is like a father and a mother. I don't know what the Aramaic word is for "mother," but in most languages the "m" sound signifies Mamma and the "b" or the "p" sound signifies Papa. So let's assume the Aramaic word is "Amma." God is like our Abba and our Amma, who push and pull us into adulthood, who then let us go but are always there, until they are not. Our heavenly Abba and Amma is *everlastingly* present, our companion, guide, and inspiration, until *we* are not. Perhaps when we are not, we are taken up into the glorious commonwealth of God's love.

PART 2

Winter Thoughts

11

Lives

Two lives are involved, my own and my wife Eva's. One thing we have in common is that we are only children. Other than that, our childhood experiences were radically different. I will tell our stories separately until the point of our unlikely first encounter.

I was born on February 26, 1934, to Jack Hodgson and Mary Crafts. They had both grown up in the Oak Park and River Forest suburbs of Chicago and attended Oak Park High School. My father went to the University of Michigan and Northwestern University, while my mother graduated from Smith College in Massachusetts. They were married in 1932, and two years later I was born. We lived in a duplex on Mapleton Avenue in Oak Park and frequently visited my grandparents: the Crafts lived a few blocks away on Scoville Avenue, and the Hodgsons lived in River Forest. My mother had a younger brother, Edward, who joined the U.S. Forest Service and eventually became its assistant director. He and his wife, Sally, had two children, Fred and Julia, who were my most proximate cousins both at the beginning and later in life. My father was the middle of three sons. His older brother had no children, and his younger brother five. Now only two of them survive, Debby Kline, who lives in Windsor, Colorado, and Judith Wainer, who lives

Part 2: Winter Thoughts

in West Palm Beach, Florida. Being an only child, I treasure my cousins.

I have few memories from the Mapleton Avenue days, but photographs exist, especially of visits with the Crafts. My grandparents rented a cottage (called Idlewild) at a resort on Magician Lake in southern Michigan; the owner was Don Gregory, one of my grandmother's cousins, and the resort, unsurprisingly, was called Gregory Beach. Grandfather Crafts died in 1939, and for the next ten years or so my family would visit Grandmother Crafts at her cottage every summer. There at the Beach a group of kids got together and had various adventures ranging from raising turtles to weenie roasts to rowing boats to playing tennis on a dirt court. These were my principal friends at this stage of life; I was a serious and introverted child.

My father, like his father and grandfather before him, worked for Continental Can Company. In the autumn of 1940 he was transferred to Memphis, Tennessee, as manager of the plant there. He found a house for us, and my mother and I moved early in 1941. The house was chosen because it was near Memphis State Teachers' College (now the University of Memphis), which had a highly regarded training school. I could walk to school by going through a back yard and following a path across open fields. The teachers there were experienced and demanding, and, since this was during the war years, few student teachers were present.

Memphis itself was a culture shock. It was part of the Old South, and only seventy-five years had passed since the end of the Civil War. People were certainly nice to us, and I had several close friends, but my parents and I always felt like what we were, Yankees. Nonetheless these were happy years for me. I had an electric train in the attic, I joined the Cub Scouts, and I read quite a bit. One of my teachers recommended the Swallows and Amazons series, by Arthur Ransome. These were stories set in the Lake District and Norfolk Broads of England. Boys and girls from two families became friendly rivals and had quite a few adventures together, including sailing, camping, and exploring. I was unaware at the time that Ransome had been a war correspondent during the Russian

Revolution and had become sympathetic with the Bolshevik cause, even marrying one of Trotsky's secretaries. I read all of the books and had to go to the Memphis Central Library to check them out.

I got to the library by walking about four blocks to the nearest bus stop and taking the bus downtown. Kids did things in those days without a sense of risk. I remember wondering to myself on more than one occasion why black people were required to ride in the back of the bus and give up their seats to white people if the bus was full. It seemed terribly unfair to me, but I never asked anyone about it, not even my parents. It was the way things were done. It didn't occur to me at the time that the libraries were also segregated, but they were and had separate entrances. Jim Crow was the harsh law of the South.

When I was eleven years old, I began riding the train from Memphis through Chicago to Niles, Michigan, where my grandmother would meet me, and with whom I would spend several weeks at Gregory Beach. In earlier years my mother would go with me, but in 1945 I went on my own for the first time. During my transfer in Chicago the newspapers had big headlines about an atomic bomb that had been dropped on Japan. I didn't know what an atomic bomb was, but it sounded very scary and apocalyptic. Then before we arrived in Niles a drunken soldier became rowdy and overly friendly toward me. I had quite a bit to tell my grandmother when I saw her. It was during these summers at Gregory Beach that I became well acquainted with my cousin Fred Crafts, two years younger than I, and less so with his younger sister, Julia. I also became good friends with Helen Jean Crider, my same age, and her extended family. Much later she and her husband, Gordon Smith, sponsored educational programs in Africa, and she became a trustee of Wesley Theological Seminary in Washington DC. Helen remembers being invited for dinner to our cottage once each summer and having to wear a dress for the occasion (my grandmother had a reputation on the Beach). We kids used to row across or walk around the lake, pick cherries and apples from the fruit trees, and ride into Dowagiac in the back of a truck for supplies, including ice for the ice boxes. We also pumped drinking

Part 2: Winter Thoughts

water from wells between the cottages, drank fresh (unpasteurized) milk, and fed garbage to the pigs.

My grandmother, Verna Harris Crafts, was one of the first women to graduate from the University of Michigan, where she met her husband, Harry, who became an attorney. By the time I spent summers with her, she was in her sixties with white hair and always seemed "old" to me. She was a fairly strict disciplinarian, but I got along well with her, stimulated and somewhat intimidated by her lively intellect. When my mother was present, things were more complicated because my mother thought I was less well-behaved than Cousin Fred. My grandmother owned a 1938 Packard, a beautiful black vehicle that she kept for a long time, storing it in the winter and driving it only in the summer. This car had the option of "freewheeling" and on country roads would roll right along without engine braking. I loved riding with my grandmother. I did not know my Hodgson grandparents as well. In the 1920s they were a glamorous family with three handsome boys, a large house on Bonnie Brae in River Forest, and Packard convertibles. My grandfather lost quite a bit in the stock market crash of 1929, and they were living in more straitened circumstances when I was born.[1] Bill and Alice Hodgson were always warm and relaxed, whereas the Crafts were more stiff and formal. My parents were more frugal than their parents, having lived through the Depression, and they passed their frugality on to me.

Our last year in Memphis was 1948. My father was transferred to the Continental Can plant in St. Louis, and we moved to University City, Missouri, in 1949. The primary advantage of our living there, as far as I was concerned, came from a contact with

---

1. A few years ago I worked on the Hodgson family history, of which my father had only vague memories. My great-grandfather, John George Hodgson, was born in Bolton, Lancashire, in 1847, but moved with his parents to Philadelphia in the early 1850s. He was trained as a machinist and in the 1870s went to Chicago where he became employed by the Continental Can Company. He held patents for much of the newly automated can-making equipment, and these made him a rather wealthy man. But he came from a humble background; his father was a leather worker and tailor, and previous generations were tenant farmers in southern Durham and north Yorkshire.

the Danforth Foundation, which operated summer camps for boys and girls in Michigan. I went to Camp Miniwanca (between Lake Michigan and Stony Lake) in 1949 and 1950 and loved it, although an earlier camping experience in North Carolina in 1947 was not a good one. My father was transferred again in 1950 to Baltimore, and we arrived as a family in January 1951. My last three high school years were spent at Baltimore City College, an all-male school and part of an old Baltimore tradition. I was assigned to a section with talented students, most of whom were Jewish.

During my high school years I became active in the youth fellowship at Govans Presbyterian Church. The youth director and associate pastor was George Landes, who came from Missouri to study for a doctorate in Semitic languages and literature at Johns Hopkins University. George and his wife, Carol, were quite stimulating for teenagers, and we had excellent discussions. These were formative years for me, including the beginning of some lifelong friendships. George went on to teach Hebrew Bible at Union Theological Seminary in New York, where he remained his entire career. When he retired, he and Carol moved to the vicinity of Allentown, Pennsylvania, which provided the opportunity of seeing them from time to time. Also during the Baltimore years my family reconnected with our Crafts relatives who had moved to Chevy Chase, Maryland.

Despite my youth fellowship interests, when I was ready to attend college I thought I wanted to be an engineer since I had worked in my father's plant for a couple of summers in the drafting department. Cornell University seemed to be the perfect place for me, but I also visited Princeton and saw its beautiful campus. So I applied to Cornell, Princeton, and Johns Hopkins. The Princeton Club of Baltimore took considerable interest in my application and urged me in the strongest terms to attend. When I received a scholarship, it settled the matter. After I began my studies I realized pretty quickly that I was not cut out for engineering. What interested me were the humanities—literature, history, philosophy, religion, classics. I majored in European history with a minor in religion.

PART 2: WINTER THOUGHTS

Princeton was a challenging social experience for me. It was still a bastion of white male privilege with only a few ethnic minorities. At least half my classmates had attended prep schools, and many were from wealthy families. My social awkwardness became evident during the spring of sophomore year when our entire class "bickered" to join an eating club. There were no other options at that time. Fortunately our class president, Coleman Brown, committed himself to insure that every student would receive at least one bid. That's what saved me and my roommate, and I have been eternally grateful since overall Princeton provided a wonderful opportunity. While it is still an elite college, it now has an amazingly diverse student body. I became involved in the Westminster Foundation at Princeton, and most of my extracurricular activities centered on its programs. Through the Foundation I became involved too in the Middle Atlantic Student Christian Movement, whose inspirational leader, Gayraud Wilmore, had a major influence on my life and later become an important African American religious thinker. Others who were important for me at this time were E. Harris Harbison (my senior thesis adviser), Bruce Morgan and Ernest Gordon (Westminster Foundation directors), and Lewis Mudge and Benjamin Reist (Princeton Seminary graduate students). During the summer before my senior year (1955) I traveled with a few fellow Student Christian Movement (SCM) students and staff members to a conference in Eagles Mere, Pennsylvania, where a program was being provided for college students working in the hotels.

Following my graduation in June 1956, I went to Europe to participate in a work camp sponsored by the World Council of Churches and the World Student Christian Federation, with which the SCM was affiliated. On the boat I met a number of work campers, including Skip Vilas, who had just graduated from Yale. Skip and I traveled together for about three weeks prior to the beginning of the camps. We started in Paris, took the train to Geneva, then on to the vicinity of the Jungfrau (Wilderswil) and to Venice. We returned to Geneva for a meeting of all the work campers at the Ecumenical Institute in Bossey, then rode the train up the Rhine to our respective camps, his in northern France, mine in Belgium. In Cologne we visited the ruins of the cathedral, which required many years to rebuild. My camp was intended to make repairs at a parish church that had been damaged during the war. Our workers came from the United States, Britain, France, Belgium, and Cuba. All this was a new, exciting, and maturing adventure for me. Skip had already decided on the Episcopal ministry. We reconnected in northern New Jersey just prior to my sixtieth reunion at Princeton in 2016.

In the spring of 1953 I attended a conference on the ministry at Union Theological Seminary. A large number of college students assembled, and we were treated to the best that Union had to offer: lectures by Reinhold Niebuhr and Paul Tillich, an evening spent with both of them, and a visit to the East Harlem Protestant Parish. I thought that ministry might be a career for me, but I was more drawn to the teaching ministry or higher education. I applied to Union and to Yale Divinity School, with its equally famous faculty. The small number of seminary-bound graduates in our Princeton class largely chose between the two institutions. Coleman Brown chose Union. I and several others chose Yale.

Yale Divinity School was in its heyday during the 1950s, with a distinguished faculty and talented students. Over the course of my seven years in New Haven, I studied under Richard Niebuhr, Robert Calhoun, Hans Frei, Claude Welch, James Gustafson, George Lindbeck, Julian Hartt, Roland Bainton, Sydney Ahlstrom, Davie Napier, Paul Minear, Paul Schubert, and Paul Meyer. During the first year I took pretty much the standard curriculum, but in the second year began to focus more on theological and New Testament studies. In the summer of 1957 I fulfilled my field education requirement as an assistant in the Dille Cooperative Parish in northeastern Pennsylvania, a Congregational ministry headquartered in LeRaysville. During the summer my parents came to visit, and I suggested they stay in Eagles Mere, with which I had become acquainted two years earlier, about thirty-five miles to the south. They were accommodated at the Forest Inn in Eagles Mere Park, near the beach, and they liked it so much that they returned

Part 2: Winter Thoughts

annually. For the first few years they stayed at the Inn, then rented cottages from it, and finally purchased their own cottage, the Mushroom, in 1966. Eagles Mere became for my family a new Magician Lake. My summer parish experience ended abruptly in late August because of a dispute with the minister in charge, and I returned to Baltimore only to discover that my father had been taken to the hospital with a heart attack.

During my second year at YDS, my field education involved working with the Westminster Foundation at Yale, which at that time was without a full-time director. Instead, three divinity students ran the program quite successfully. At the end of the year I was invited to serve as a seminar leader at the annual summer conference of the New England Student Christian Movement, with which the Westminster Foundation was affiliated. The conference took place at Camp O-At-Ka, on Sebago Lake in Maine, from June 9 to 15, 1958. The topic for this year was "The Courage to Act," and the platform speakers were David Carmichael from Ghana, West Africa, and a lay member of the Iona Community; Eberhard Bethge, editor of the writings of Dietrich Bonhoeffer and a lecturer at Harvard Divinity School; and Maynard Catchings, National Student YMCA staff member for interracial and intercultural programming. It was a high-powered conference and an amazing experience.

My discussion group met for first time on Tuesday, June 10, on rocks by the lakeshore. Among its members was a young woman who had completed her second year at Wellesley College and who spoke with only a slightly discernible accent: Eva Sara Fornady. She was fluent in German, had just spent a year studying biblical history with Leander Keck, and knew about Barth, Bonhoeffer, Bultmann, and other German theologians. She led a very moving vespers service on Thursday evening. On Saturday I offered her a ride home to New Jersey; she had made other arrangements but had a premonition that I would write.

Now it is time to tell Eva's story up to this point. She was born on March 28, 1937, in Budapest, Hungary, the daughter of Bubik Sára and Fornády Tibor. It was Easter Sunday, and a family dinner had to be interrupted by a sudden trip to the hospital. Her parents lived in an apartment on the Buda hills. Her father worked in the directorate of the Hungarian State Railroad, and her mother was a music education teacher. The Fornády family was of old German nobility and came to Hungary several centuries earlier; they still used the German name "Fischer" until the mid-1930s, when they assumed the name of the Hungarian community, Fornád, where their ancestors first settled. Eva's maternal grandparents were Bubik Lajos and Tóth Gabriella. They were married in 1911 in Almádi, on Lake Balaton, but Lajos died in 1916 during the First World War, about a year and a half after his daughter, Sára, was born. Gabriella moved to Bicske where she was employed as an elementary school teacher and raised Sára. She wrote down the family histories of the Fornády, Bubik, Tóth and Kiss families from memory and gave the memoir to Eva in 1960.[2] Her best memories were of the Tóths and Kisses and went back several generations. Her mother Kiss Jólan had six children by her first marriage and two by her second, serving all the while as a full-time teacher. Her grandmother (Eva's great-great-grandmother) Iklódi nemes Soós Mária, who married Kiss Daniel, was the only member of her large family to survive the bubonic plague in 1848 and later owned a vineyard and summer home in Almádi overlooking her beloved Balaton where members of the extended family gathered. The years following the First World War were very difficult for Grandmother Bubik; her family was expelled by the Serbs from its home in Hodosány, an ethnic Croatian area. There were severe food shortages and rampant inflation; little Sára was taken to Switzerland to recuperate. Later they inherited property in Almádi and in 1927 built a cabin called Kis Tanya (Little Camp), where they spent summers near the lake during the 1930s. This is where Sára and Tibor met.

Hungary joined the Second World War on the side of Germany, Austria, and Italy. The reasons for this included the historic

---

2. The memoir was written in Hungarian. Eva translated it when we were preparing to visit her Hungarian relatives in 1996. Hungarian accents and name order are used only in this paragraph.

alliance between Austria and Hungary, the fascist tendencies of the Horthy regime, and the aftermath of the Treaty of Trianon (1920), which deprived the country of over two-thirds of its territory and over three million ethnic Hungarians. This treaty stirred great resentment, as did the Treaty of Versailles in Germany, where it bred economic and social conditions that nourished the growth of National Socialism. In 1943 the Hungarian government tried to negotiate a secret peace with the Allies, but to stop the defection German troops entered the country in 1944, and Budapest was partly destroyed by fighting between the Germans and the Soviets. At this time the mass deportation of Hungarian Jews began, mainly to Auschwitz.

In the fall of 1944 Eva and her grandmother left Budapest and moved to Almadi, where they were joined later by her mother; her father stayed behind partly because there were tensions in the marriage. When the fighting approached Lake Balaton, they traveled with other family members to Szombathely on the Austrian border. As Soviet troops advanced, they crossed the border on Eva's eighth birthday, March 28, 1945, and made their way by train to the town of Itling in Bavaria, where the tracks were bombed out in both directions. The lived on the train for a while, then in the attic of a nearby farm house, until Sara Fornady was able to arrange, through an acquaintance in Stuttgart, for them to be settled in the village of Neckartailfingen in Württemberg as war refugees. Eva soon became fluent in German. Like her mother, she visited friends in Switzerland in 1948.

Following the war Hungary became a satellite state of the Soviet Union. Word arrived that Eva's father had been granted a divorce and remarried. If Eva returned to Hungary, the threat existed that he would seek custody and she would be separated from her mother. This, combined with the appalling political and economic conditions in their homeland, led Sara Fornady to decide on emigration to the USA since they could not remain permanently in Germany. To be eligible they had to move to a refugee camp in Stuttgart–Bad Cannstatt. Finally, the required sponsorship came from a church in Syracuse, New York. In June 1950 Eva, her mother and grandmother, traveled by ship to Boston, then by train to Syracuse. She was thirteen years old. This is the same year I moved to Baltimore with my parents. Our paths were slowly converging.

Eva attended Onondaga Valley High School and quickly learned English. Because of the harsh winter climate in Syracuse, the family moved two years later to Boston, where Sara Fornady had made the acquaintance of a volunteer with Church World Service, Amy Clark, who had met their boat and with whom she had corresponded. A confusion about school districts led to Eva's living with Amy Clark and her husband during the week so she could attend Newton High School. There she excelled as an industrious immigrant, becoming editor of the school newspaper and the senior yearbook. She planned to attend Elmhurst College, which was one of the few institutions offering a major in Hungarian (essentially her mother's idea). But a high school guidance counselor insisted in no uncertain terms that instead she would attend nearby Wellesley College, for which she was amply qualified. Wellesley provided a scholarship that covered all her expenses, and the matter was settled. She entered in 1956, a few months after becoming an American citizen. In the meantime her mother had married Istvan Angyal, an architect who had studied in Italy and spent the war years in North Africa, escaping the fate of most of his family, who died in concentration camps. He moved to Boston because his brother Andras, a psychiatrist, was already there. At Wellesley Eva studied a broad field of subjects and decided on a major in German. She became active in the college chapel, the Wesley Foundation of Cambridge, and the Student Christian Movement of New England. That's why she attended the conference at O-At-Ka in June 1958.

Eva and I began corresponding in the summer of 1958. She was employed as a counselor at the Herald Tribune Fresh Air Camp near Bear Mountain, New York, and I was working with underprivileged kids at a community center in Baltimore, so we had some common experiences to share.[3] We arranged a date at

---

3. Eva charmed me when she wrote: "And so goes life at Sunny Ledge,

Part 2: Winter Thoughts

the end of summer when I would be returning to Yale Divinity School. I drove to her home in Bergenfield, New Jersey, and then into Manhattan, where we found a French restaurant and attended a performance of *Look Homeward, Angel*. Upon returning home, I met her mother at 2:00 a.m. and we had coffee and cake before I continued on to New Haven.

During the fall semester I roomed with Georg Dellbrügge, a student from Germany who had completed a divinity degree at the Oberlin School of Theology and was just beginning a PhD program in social ethics with Richard Niebuhr. Eva and I next saw each other on the weekend of October 18. The visit was quite successful and we began planning our next get-together for the weekend of November 15–16, when Princeton would play Yale in football. My college roommate, Dick Baker, was coming for the event, and Eva brought her roommate, Nancy May, as a date. I told Georg that he too should have a date. Georg went to the Graduate School and asked for a list of German female graduate students. He interviewed several women and settled on Sybille von Bülow, who was beginning a program in Slavic Languages. She had come to the United States about six years earlier as an au pair and was subsequently sponsored at Bryn Mawr College by a Philadelphia family. Georg and Sybille began seeing each other nearly every day after that weekend. To the astonishment of everyone, they were married six weeks later (December 19) in Dwight Chapel on the Yale campus. In the meantime Eva had invited me to visit her at Wellesley on December 5–6, and that's when we realized we were falling in love. She came to New Haven for the wedding, following which we drove to Bergenfield where I was treated to an elaborate Hungarian dinner. During the Christmas holidays she visited me in Baltimore, where my father made her eat raw oysters. From then on, of course, we were dating steadily, and became informally engaged on my birthday, February 26. So things moved very

---

as I am motherly to runaways, contend with gang leaders, get stung by bugs, find worms crawling in my new toothbrush, attempt to make dreary duties sound glamorous, go fishing with a stick, string, and safety pin . . . oddities ad infinitum, a summer forever to be remembered."

quickly for us. Despite our vastly different childhood experiences and personality contrasts, we had important interests and values in common. We were married in the Yale Divinity School Chapel on June 18, 1960, three weeks after Eva's graduation from Wellesley. Professor Claude Welch, who had married the Dellbrügges, did the same for us.

During my senior year at Yale Divinity School (1958–59), I took a seminar with Paul Schubert on Paul's Epistles to the Corinthians. In our discussion of the first chapter of First Corinthians, I learned how Ferdinand Christian Baur discovered his famous thesis about the opposition between two factions in Corinth, a Jewish-Christian party (Peter) and a Gentile-Christian party (Paul). This in turn led to other breakthrough discoveries in New Testament research by Baur, who became the greatest historical theologian of the nineteenth century. Baur sounded like a fascinating figure, but to study him further I would have to learn German. I had begun to study the language on my own, and in the summer of 1959 enrolled for a crash course at the Yale Summer Language Institute. This in turn led to the idea of spending a year in Germany. My proposal to Eva was couched in terms of my asking whether she would like to go to Germany with me.

Reality dictated that we not do so. After our marriage and the beginning of my PhD studies at Yale in modern theology, we needed money to live on. After earning a Master of Arts in Teaching at Yale,[4] Eva was employed as a language instructor at Southern Connecticut State College in New Haven. On the first day she was confronted with the expectation that she teach not only German but also a beginning class in French. She had studied French for three years in high school but not in college. Fortunately she was adept at languages and managed quite well, but the following summer she enrolled in an advanced French course at the Language Institute. This proved quite useful later on, but she never taught French again.

---

4. Eva gave up a career as a college language teacher to be with me. She was encouraged by the Department of German at Yale to continue on for a PhD, but she decided it was impractical.

Part 2: Winter Thoughts

I settled into writing my dissertation on Baur, under the direction of the brilliant Hans Frei, and I completed my PhD in June 1963. Shortly thereafter Eva and I departed on our first trip to Germany, where we spent the summer studying Baur manuscripts in the University of Tübingen Library. We made a few excursions, including stops in London and Paris, an overnight rail trip to Rome and Florence, and another to Munich. Prior to our departure we attended the wedding of Eva's college roommate, Nancy May, to Jim Pratt. Jim was a friend of mine at Yale Divinity School, and we arranged their first date. Jim served forty years as the pastor of the Noank Baptist Church on the coast of Connecticut, and, after a fifteen-year hiatus near London following his retirement, Nancy and Jim returned to Noank in 2016 and now live about a block from their former parsonage.

Upon our return from Germany Eva and I experienced culture shock as we drove to San Antonio, Texas, for my first job as an assistant professor of religion at Trinity University, a Presbyterian-related college. Eva taught German part-time at San Antonio Junior College, but she was expecting our first child, David, who was born May 1, 1964. We remained in San Antonio for another year, and then I was fortunate to be offered a position at the Divinity School of Vanderbilt University in the spring of 1965.

The Divinity School faculty was in a rebuilding phase at that time. Five years earlier, the School was shaken when one of its students, James Lawson, was expelled by the Board of Trust for leading the Nashville sit-in movement, which involved nonviolent resistance. Lawson was already well known, a follower of Gandhi and Martin Luther King Jr. Most of the faculty resigned, and protests followed in other parts of the University. A settlement was finally reached that reinstated Lawson and allowed him to complete his degree in absentia.[5] This led to considerable faculty and administrative turnover during the next few years. Jack Forstman was appointed as successor to Langdon Gilkey, Ray Hart as

---

5. Lawson returned to Vanderbilt Divinity School for a D.Min. degree in 1970, and about thirty years later he was honored by the University as a distinguished alumnus, following which he served as a visiting scholar.

successor to Gordon Kaufman, and Robert Funk as successor to Kendrick Grobel. I learned quite a bit from my senior colleagues, especially about the so-called "new hermeneutic" advanced by Gerhard Ebeling and others.

Ebeling came to Vanderbilt as a visiting professor in 1968, and he offered me use of his study in the Institute for Hermeneutics at the University of Tübingen in 1968–69 because he himself had accepted a call to the University of Zürich. So our family, which had been expanded by the arrival of Jennifer on January 3, 1967, moved to Tübingen for my first leave of absence. During 1968–69 about fifty Americans in the field of religion, Catholics and Protestants, were studying or doing research at Tübingen. We had weekly luncheons at the Museum Restaurant and gatherings of the Ausländercolloquium with presentations by Hans Küng, Ernst Käsemann, Jürgen Moltmann, and other distinguished Tübingen scholars. Eva became active in the German-American Women's Club, and we made frequent trips in the vicinity and a few longer ones, including to Berlin where we visited Georg and Sybille Dellbrügge and their four children. Georg at that time was director of the Johannesstift and had contacts in East Berlin. It was a momentous year because we arrived in Germany on the day of the Soviet invasion of Czechoslovakia, and East-West theological conversations were disrupted. In the spring I visited Prague with a German university student group. Later in the spring, student protests and strikes shut down much of Tübingen and other universities.

We have revisited Germany many times, most recently in late autumn 2017 with a church-sponsored group commemorating the five-hundredth anniversary of the Reformation. We started in Berlin and ended in Heidelberg, with visits to Magdeburg, Wittenberg, Leipzig, Eisleben, Erfurt, and Eisenach. All of these Luther-related towns are in former East Germany, and it was good to see how successfully this whole area has been rebuilt. In Erfurt at the Augustinian monastery Luther entered in 1505, Eva and I led a brief devotion and reflected on the similarities and differences between Luther and Bonhoeffer, whose memorial we visited in Berlin. Both were courageous leaders and brilliant thinkers, but Luther amplified the "background noise" of anti-Semitism in late-medieval culture with his infamous diatribe against the Jews (1543),[6] whereas Bonhoeffer steadfastly resisted the nationalism, fascism, and anti-Semitism of his own culture, which made him very much a prophetic figure and a martyr to the truth.

When I returned to Vanderbilt in the summer of 1969, several new appointments had been made: Edward Farley in theology (successor to Ray Hart); Eugene TeSelle in church history (with then spouse Sallie McFague); Howard Harrod and Thomas Ogletree in ethics. A few years later Sallie McFague was offered a teaching position, and in 1975 she became the dean of Vanderbilt Divinity School. In 1971 Ogletree and I taught a course on Theology and the Black Experience with the help of Kelly Miller Smith and James Lawson. This was another transformative experience for me, and a couple of years later the School appointed its first fulltime black professor, Peter Paris, in ethics. In 1974 Leander Keck (who joined the Vanderbilt faculty following his time at Wellesley) and I taught jointly a seminar on Nineteenth Century Lives of Jesus. The next year Keck left for Candler School of Theology and eventually Yale Divinity School, serving as dean in both institutions. By the early 1970s the Vanderbilt faculty had assembled a group that worked together in theology for over a quarter of a century. We achieved an international reputation and attracted many excellent graduate students. Among these, especially in the 1970s, were a number of Catholics, who at that time were being encouraged to seek graduate degrees from non-Catholic institutions. New Testament professor John Donahue, SJ, helped to recruit them, and quite a few studied in his field. Our theology-ethics graduates

6. The Topography of Terror Museum in Berlin (on the site of the former Gestapo/SS/Reich Security headquarters) held a special exhibit in October 2017 showing how Luther's writings were used by the Nazis to advance their cause. The Town Church in Wittenberg where Luther was married and preached has preserved a *Judensau* gargoyle as evidence of anti-Semitism, with a Jewish memorial below. Ronald S. Lauder, president of the World Jewish Congress, said recently: "More than any other country, Germany has faced up to the crimes of its past in an honest and straightforward way, and has made it clear at the highest levels of government that the memory of the Holocaust must never be forgotten or diminished." *New York Times*, January 11, 2018, A4.

LIVES

included Dan Jamros (Buffalo), Paul Lakeland (Fairfield), Edward Malloy and Oliver Williams (Notre Dame), William McConville (Siena and Raleigh), Mary Aquin O'Neill (Baltimore), and Bill Reiser (Holy Cross). We also had many stellar Protestant graduates: David Fisher (North Central College), Wendy Farley (Emory, San Francisco Seminary), Mary Fulkerson (Duke), David Jensen (Austin Seminary), Hyo-Dong Lee (Drew Theological School), Anselm Min (Claremont), Darby Ray (Bates), Tom Reynolds (Toronto), John Shelley (Clemson), Melissa Stewart (Adrian), George Stroup (Columbia Seminary), Sigurdur Thordarson (Reykjavik), Deanna Thompson (Hamline), Sharon Welch (Meadville Lombard Theological School), to name a few with whom I have stayed in touch. During my thirty-eight years at Vanderbilt, I taught courses on Protestant theology in the nineteenth century, contemporary theology, constructive and systematic theology, liberation theology, christology, Trinity, creation and providence, theology and world religions, Hegel, Barth, Tillich, Rahner—again to name just a few. Who could have asked for a better opportunity than the one I had?

In 1977 Eva was first employed by the Metropolitan Schools of Nashville and Davidson County as an ESL teacher. She excelled as a teacher and continued for twenty-five years until her retirement in 2002. I retired the following year, in 2003. In 2004 we started traveling with Elderhostel / Road Scholar and have benefited from their programs in Hawaii, California, Oregon, Arizona, Utah, New Mexico, Nova Scotia, Ireland, France, Italy, Greece, Hungary, Czech Republic, and Poland. In the same year we became summer-long residents of Eagles Mere, having inherited the cottage my parents purchased in 1966. We had visited them many times in prior years, and, following my mother's death in 1994, I spent most of the summer with my father until his death in 2003. My cousin Fred Crafts moved to Eagles Mere as a permanent resident when he retired, and his sister, Julia (now Julie), and her husband Paul Kaminski built a cottage in the 1980s. We enjoyed many summers together and had family gatherings, but in recent years both Fred and Julie have been in poor health. One of Eva's and my favorite activities in Eagles Mere is called Brain/Food, a program of potlucks followed by discussions of books, films, and plays. Eagles Mere Friends of the Arts sponsors a summer series, and I can engage in some of my favorite activities: walking, tennis, sailing, swimming. We have many summer friends and keep busy, even during quiet times.

Our daughter, Jennifer, turned fifty in 2017, and David is three years older, so they are now both in middle age. David lives in Nashville, is married to Brenda Batey, and is an independent contractor with numerous local clients. Jennifer lives in Arvada, Colorado, a suburb of Denver, with her husband, Tom Anton, who is an engineer with Suncor, a Canadian energy company. They have two boys adopted from Guatemala, Christopher and Nicholas, our only grandchildren. Jennifer is employed as a counseling psychologist and consultant.

I was raised as a Presbyterian and Eva in the Reformed Church of Hungary. Her father was Catholic but her mother was Reformed, and a daughter followed the religion of her mother. My father was Episcopalian and my mother Presbyterian, but he joined the Presbyterian Church after their marriage. The Reformed tradition suits me well because of its motto, *ecclesia reformata et semper reformanda*: the "always reforming" part expresses what I refer to below as the Protestant principle. But many of the thinkers I have been influenced by are Lutheran, and some are Catholic, so my theological convictions are not just typical of those found among Presbyterians. I am also committed to a serious dialogue among world religions. We attend a church in Nashville with an excellent Reformed liturgy and strong pastoral leadership.

Eva and I have lived into our eighties and are fortunate to be in relatively good health. As we grow older, more of our friends have passed away. Among them are colleagues from the Divinity School: Liston Mills, Howard Harrod, Dale Johnson, Jack Forstman, Edward Farley, David Buttrick, and Gene TeSelle. Others are in poor health, so my conversation partners are gone. Among friends in Eagles Mere, our most recent loss is David Leverenz, the leader of Brain/Food for many years and a retired professor of English at Florida State University. My cousin Fred Crafts has died, and his sister Julie is in a nursing facility. These deaths and illnesses remind us of our mortality, and, as I said to my classmates at Princeton, mortality must be recognized as part of the cycle of life. If old life did not pass away, new life would be impossible, and the earth would be choked by its own fecundity. The brevity of human life heightens its beauty and pathos. Belief in the immortality of the soul strikes me as implausible, because a disembodied soul would have no identity and specificity. I believe rather that our individual lives are taken back into the eternal life of God, where we continue as part of a greater corporate existence but not as individual beings. This is a mystery we cannot fathom. We live on through our thoughts, deeds, and contributions to the greater good, but to perpetuate an individual consciousness into eternity seems pointless and cruel.

12

Theologies

I began reading theology in college. Although my major was European history, I took courses on modern religious and ethical thought and seminars on topics such as Augustine and Kierkegaard.[1] The first two theologians I read seriously were Reinhold Niebuhr and Paul Tillich. Niebuhr's *The Nature and Destiny of Man* first appeared in 1941 and 1943 as two volumes of Gifford Lectures, and then in a one-volume edition in 1949. It made Niebuhr an important public intellectual, who is still quoted today by columnists like David Brooks, and the book had an enormous impact on a whole generation of students and scholars. Niebuhr was a "Christian realist" who brought tough critiques to bear on rationalism, romanticism, and idealism, but also on orthodoxy and literalism. He virtually coined the term "neo-orthodoxy," which was influenced by Karl Barth's dialectical theology but was also quite independent of it. For me the book was a first exposure to countless names, figures, and issues in modern theology, and I devoured it hungrily. Later I discovered that Niebuhr was

---

1. The seminar on Augustine and Kierkegaard was taught by Professor Paul Ramsey, who would sometimes get carried away with rhetorical enthusiasm as he spoke on topics of deep concern. He is best known for his *Basic Christian Ethics* (1950), which I read in college.

overly facile in posing oppositions (such as between the classical, Christian, and modern views of "man") and making sweeping generalizations, for which he was criticized by more careful scholars. But his books also provided explanations of the truly tragic events that occurred in the first half of the twentieth century. As a major in history and with an interest in interpretations of history, I was especially engaged by Niebuhr's *Faith and History: A Comparison of Christian and Modern Views of History* (1949), and *The Irony of American History* (1952). Most of Niebuhr's books originated as lectures at colleges and seminaries, and he was in great demand as a public speaker. I met him for the first and only time in March 1953 when I attend the Union Theological Seminary Conference on the Ministry.

Paul Tillich was the greatest Protestant theologian, along with Karl Barth, in the twentieth century. He was teaching at the University of Frankfurt in 1933 when Hitler became German Chancellor. Tillich was dismissed because of his oppositional stance and accepted an offer from Reinhold Niebuhr to join the faculty of Union Theological Seminary, where he taught from 1933 to 1955. I began reading Tillich in college, starting with *The Protestant Era* (1948), a collection of essays written over the preceding twenty years. These are powerful essays, introducing concepts such as "kairos" and "the Protestant principle," and organized into sections on religion and history, religion and culture, religion and ethics, Protestantism and the present crisis. The "and" expresses Tillich's "method of correlation," which means that he was constantly seeking to correlate basic religious and philosophical concepts with various aspects of human experience and culture. He derived this method from early studies of Schelling and Hegel as well as twentieth-century existentialist philosophy. Faith, he wrote, is

> the state of mind in which we are grasped by the power of something unconditional which manifests itself to us as the ground and judge of our existence. The power grasping us in the state of faith is not a being beside others, not even the highest; it is not an object among objects, not even the greatest; but it is a quality of beings and

Part 2: Winter Thoughts

objects, the quality of pointing beyond themselves and their finite existence to the infinite, inexhaustible, and unapproachable depth of their being and meaning. The Protestant principle is the expression of this relationship. It is the guardian against the attempts of the finite and conditioned to usurp the place of the unconditional in thinking and acting. It is the prophetic judgment against religious pride, ecclesiastical arrogance, and secular self-sufficiency and their destructive consequences.[2]

These words made a deep impression on me and have shaped my understanding of Protestantism ever since. Later I learned that the concept of the Protestant principle goes back at least to Baur, who formulated it in different terms but with similar intent. I also read Tillich's *The Courage to Be* (1952), which dealt with the problem of being, nonbeing, and anxiety; and a collection of sermons, *The Shaking of the Foundations* (1948). I had formed a Niebuhrian and Tillichian worldview by the time I graduated from college.

All of my studies at Princeton—in history, religion, philosophy, literature, social sciences—taught me the discipline of critical thinking. Critical thinking means that no claims can be based on appeals to authority, that all truths must be tested through differences of interpretation, and that our knowledge of truth is always relative to our circumstances and interests. This does not mean that truth is unknowable, but that it is knowable only relatively. Relativity is very different from relativism. The universal is present, but only concretely, in the myriad events and thoughts of history. Constructing an interpretation of history can take a lifetime. Once you have learned the discipline of critical thinking, you can never return to naïve belief or unexamined allegiances. It is the greatest gift a college education can give you. The specific details and contents of your education fade away, but the discipline remains.

Tillich left Union Seminary in 1955 to become a university professor at Harvard, and Reinhold Niebuhr was planning to retire a few years later. That's one reason why I chose Yale Divinity School. At that time the Yale faculty was absorbing the influence of Karl

---

2. Tillich, *The Protestant Era*, 163.

THEOLOGIES

Barth, whose *Church Dogmatics* began to appear in English translation in 1956. The first half-volume, *The Doctrine of the Word of God*, actually came out twenty years earlier, but the Second World War interrupted the translation project, which could be resumed only in the 1950s with a team of mostly Scottish scholars and pastors. Altogether the work encompassed 13 volumes and took another decade to be completed in English. It was based on lectures delivered by Barth at the University of Basel over many years. The lectures themselves were interspersed with smaller-print sections caused "excursuses," which contained detailed historical references and theological arguments, and were often the most fascinating part of the whole. The excursuses were much indebted to the work of Charlotte von Kirschbaum, who was Barth's secretary, muse, and theological assistant for over three decades. During my years at Yale I read a great deal of Barth, and it is fair to say that I became a Barthian. There is something seductive about Barth's worldview and his dialectical theology, threading its way beyond liberal and orthodox positions to constant affirmations of the primacy of God and God's Word over all human undertakings, yet acknowledging that God's Word can only be heard through human words and interpreted by human thinking. In this he was similar to Niebuhr and Tillich, but his convictions as a Swiss Reformed theologian gave his theology a different, more Calvinist hue.

Barth was influenced by Swiss religious socialists, who attuned him to political issues. He was shocked when one of his liberal teachers, Adolf von Harnack, signed a manifesto of German intellectuals in support of the war policy of Kaiser Wilhelm—a policy that, along with the folly of Austria, led to one of the most futile conflicts in human history and a tragic aftermath, the rise of Nazism and an even more terrible second war. Barth taught in German universities during the 1920s and 1930s, until he refused to swear allegiance to Hitler and authored the Barmen Declaration, which became the basis for the Confessing Church. At this time Barth returned to Switzerland and became a professor at Basel. This background gave Barth's work very much a prophetic quality.

Part 2: Winter Thoughts

The professors at Yale who most influenced me in the direction of Barth were Hans Frei and George Lindbeck, and to a lesser extent Claude Welch. H. Richard Niebuhr, Reinhold Niebuhr's younger brother, was more wary of Barth, as he was of all theologians. He was a deeper, more complex, and less popular thinker than Reinhold, and probably the greatest theologian at Yale since Jonathan Edwards. I took several courses and seminars with him. He was a demanding teacher, who expected his graduate students to struggle with the difficult German of the early Schleiermacher. At the time I knew him he was working on a theology of language influenced by Michael Polanyi. He was indeed indebted to Barth for his critique of liberal theology, and he is sometimes credited with inaugurating a new postliberal school of theology, but I think that claim is misleading. Niebuhr was also appreciative of liberalism, especially in its more prophetic forms such as that found in Ernst Troeltsch. And he shied away from any kind of "school" identity. He saw the strengths and weaknesses in all positions, but believed that God claims the loyalty of human beings beyond all relativities.

Niebuhr's most influential books were *The Meaning of Revelation* (1941), dedicated to his teachers Douglas Clyde Macintosh and Frank Chamberlain Porter, and *Christ and Culture* (1951). In the latter work he developed a famous typology of the relations between Christ and culture: Christ against culture, the Christ of culture, Christ above culture, Christ and culture in paradox, and Christ the transformer of culture. While he found value in all the types, he was most attracted to the last, where he discussed the conversion motif in the Fourth Gospel and Augustine, and the views of the nineteenth-century Anglican scholar Frederick Denison Maurice. Of Maurice he wrote:

> The time of the conflict is now; the time of Christ's victory is now. We are not dealing with human progress in culture, but with the divine conversion of the spirit of man from which all culture rises. "The kingdom of God begins within, but it is to make itself manifest without. . . . It is to penetrate the feelings, habits, thoughts,

words, acts, of him who is the subject of it. At last it is to penetrate our whole social existence." The kingdom of God is transformed culture, because it is first of all the conversion of the human spirit from faithlessness and self-service to the knowledge and service of God. This kingdom is real, for if God did not rule nothing would exist; and if He had not heard the prayer for the coming of the kingdom, the world of mankind would long ago have became a den of robbers. Every moment and period is an eschatological present, for in every moment men are dealing with God.[3]

This was vintage Niebuhr.

Claude Welch taught a two-semester course on modern theology (nineteenth and twentieth century) that was a must for theology students. I took several of his seminars, including one on the Protestant liberal theologians (Ritschl, Harnack, Herrmann, Rauschenbusch), which helped to moderate my Barthian prejudices. With George Lindbeck I remember a seminar on Late Scholasticism and Luther (Duns Scotus, William of Ockham, John Wycliffe, and others who led up to Luther); it was only later that Lindbeck became one of the major authors of postliberal theology with his book *The Nature of Doctrine* (1984). Hans Frei was a brilliant thinker and compassionate human being, who arrived from Germany with his parents and experienced a conversion to Christianity. I knew him quite well because he supervised my dissertation, and we had many fascinating conversations. Other professors at Yale who influenced me were Robert Calhoun, whose lectures on the history of Christian doctrine were legendary; Julian Hartt, a philosophical theologian who forged his own path from a diversity of sources; and James Gustafson, a theological ethicist who taught his students that the church's treasure is always found only in earthen vessels. I studied with the three Pauls of the New Testament faculty: Paul Meyer, Paul Minear, and Paul Schubert.

It was from Paul Schubert, as I mentioned earlier, that I first learned about Ferdinand Christian Baur (1792–1860). Baur had a

---

3. Niebuhr, *Christ and Culture*, 228–29.

major impact in New Testament studies, even though his primary field was church history and the history of Christian thought. His breakthrough came when he discovered that, beneath the surface of the Pauline epistles, a conflict exists between opposing interpretations of the Christian gospel—a conflict between Paul himself, who, though a Jew, found himself called to be an apostle to the Gentiles, and the Jewish Christians of Jerusalem, of whom Peter was the major representative, and for whom circumcision was a requirement for participation in the community of faith. Baur demonstrated that this conflict is smoothed over in the Acts of the Apostles, and that consequently the book of Acts is not a reliable source for information about early Christianity. This in turn led to Baur's identification of criteria for distinguishing the authentic Pauline epistles from the Deutero-Pauline ones. In 1835, the same year that David Friedrich Strauss's *Life of Jesus* appeared, Baur published a controversial book arguing that the Pastoral Epistles could not have been written by the Apostle Paul. He allowed only four epistles to be genuinely Pauline: Galatians, First and Second Corinthians, and Romans; and from them he reconstructed the complex edifice of Pauline theology, as presented in his book on Paul and his lectures on New Testament theology. Baur then turned his attention to the Gospels. It became evident to him in the early 1840s that the Gospel of John is fundamentally different from the other three gospels (the Synoptic Gospels) and cannot be harmonized with them. Historical truth can be found only on the side of the Synoptics, and in Baur's judgment the sayings of Jesus are most reliably preserved in the Gospel of Matthew, even though it displays distinctive "tendencies" reflective of the interests and point of view of its author. Indeed, this is true of all the New Testament writings, and "tendency criticism" became the hallmark of Baur's method. All this was highly controversial at the time, but it made Baur the greatest New Testament scholar of the nineteenth century.

Three figures stand out for Baur in the New Testament: Jesus, Paul, and John (the unknown author of the Fourth Gospel). Jesus is the sine qua non, the one whose moral-religious teaching produces a revolution in human consciousness, and to whom Christians have always returned shorn of dogmatic assumptions. Paul shifts the focus from the teaching to the person of Christ, is the first to recognize the significance of his death for defining his messianic role, works out a complex understanding of justification by faith, and universalizes Christianity to include Gentiles as well as Jews. John provides a metaphysical foundation for Pauline universalism, and reorients redemption away from justification and grace to being made a new being in Christ, defined by love as the essential nature of God. But the Johannine achievement comes at a price, such as an antipathy toward the Jews, the evaporation of the necessity of historical mediation, and the surrender of the human person of Jesus to the divinity of the Logos. All subsequent developments in Christian theology go back to these three figures.

I was fascinated by what I was learning about Baur, and when I discovered that no major works on him had been published in English, I decided to make him the topic of my doctoral dissertation. In addition to his New Testament studies, I had to examine his major monographs in the history of Christian theology, the three volumes of his lectures on the history of Christian dogma, and the five volumes of his history of the Christian church—all in German except for his book on Paul and the first volume of the church history. I had to acquaint myself with the thinkers who had the greatest influence on Baur: Friedrich Schelling, Friedrich Schleiermacher, and Georg Wilhelm Friedrich Hegel. I had already taken extensive notes on Schleiermacher's *Christian Faith*, but Schelling and Hegel presented quite a challenge.

While I was still in college, I took a course on nineteenth-century philosophy taught by Jacob Taubes, a visiting Jewish scholar. Without any explanation whatsoever, Taubes began the first day of class by quoting the opening paragraph to chapter 7 of Hegel's *Phenomenology of Spirit*:

> In the configurations hitherto considered—which are distinguished as *consciousness, self-consciousness, reason,* and *spirit—religion* also, as the consciousness of *absolute being* in general, has doubtless made its appearance. But

Part 2: Winter Thoughts

that was from the *point of view of the consciousness* that is conscious of absolute being. But absolute being *in and for itself*, the self-consciousness of spirit, has not appeared in those forms.[4]

Taubes claimed that this summary is the key to the whole of modern philosophy, and he spent most of the fall semester expounding it, and related Hegel texts. Only in December, so he claimed, did he discover that this was a one-semester class, not two semesters, so he raced through the remainder of the nineteenth century in the final three weeks. That was my introduction to Hegel. I found his work overwhelming, mysterious, and seductive. I learned that the Lectures on the Philosophy of Religion was the principal Hegel source for Baur, and I read it in translation, but did not achieve a true understanding of it until much later. Basically I relied on Baur's reading of Hegel.

In addition to his dialectical approach to history, by which differences are resolved through ever-new mediations, it was principally Hegel's concept of God as absolute spirit that was of critical importance to Baur. He argued that this concept represents a "necessary progression" beyond Schleiermacher's feeling of utter dependence, which rightly turns to the subject but cannot regain the object. Baur summarizes Hegel's contribution as follows:

> Christianity is the self-explicating absolute idea itself. The absolute idea is God as absolute spirit, mediating itself with itself in the process of thinking. Thus Christianity is essentially this process itself, is the life process of God that explicates itself in thinking as the nature of spirit. If the content of Christianity is essentially the doctrine of the triune God, then the Trinity, as the essence of God, is the essence of spirit itself insofar as spirit, thinking itself, can relate itself to itself in no other way than in the relationship of these three elements. At this point we accordingly reach what must be regarded as the proper goal of the development of dogma from its very beginning, the inwardizing of dogma—released from its externality,

---

4. G. W. F. Hegel, *Phänomenologie des Geistes*, 473 (my translation; italics in the original). ET: *Phenomenology of Spirit*, 410.

discerned in the essence of spirit itself, and recognized as identical with spirit.... Christian consciousness itself is simply the subjective side of the absolute spirit that, in the process of mediation with itself, makes itself determinate as subjective consciousness. In a word, Christianity is not merely consciousness or feeling, but instead is thinking, is eternal thought as the self-determination of spirit, the self-movement of the concept.[5]

I had many debates with my dissertation adviser, Hans Frei, about passages like this. Frei was attracted to this aspect of Hegel's philosophy (and Baur's theology) because it emphasized the primacy of God and God's self-mediation in the world, just as Karl Barth did. But Frei was concerned that these ideas derived ultimately from a philosophical logic rather than the revelation of the biblical God. He thought that Hegel placed his loyalty in absolute spirit rather than in Jesus Christ, and that his absolute spirit is not sufficiently distinguished from the human spirit. I, however, found myself being drawn away from a strictly Barthian perspective to a more serious engagement with nineteenth-century speculative theology, which was too easily caricatured by later liberal Protestantism and then by twentieth-century critics. If there truly was to be a mutually transformative relationship between Christ and culture, this seemed to me to be a prime example of it. One of the questions I had about Niebuhr was whether he intended the transformation to run from Christ *to* culture, or to occur between Christ *and* culture. I began to worry about Barth's scriptural authoritarianism and his christocentrism, which excluded historical relativity and other possible revelations of sacred power and mystery. I was attracted to Baur's understanding of the relationship between philosophy, religion, and history, which is best summed up in the following passage:

> What would the metaphysical truth be without its historical mediation, if it did not actualize itself in the

---

5. Baur, *History of Christian Dogma*, 335. The "three elements" of the Trinity are Father, Son, and Spirit; or in philosophical categories, identity, difference, and mediation.

consciousness of humanity by appearing in history, and doing so not merely in scattered individuals but in the organic nexus of historical development, thus emerging out of the abstract region of philosophy into the concrete life of religion, and becoming part of the collective consciousness of a religious and ecclesial community? And what, on the other hand, would the historical aspect be—everything that has objectified itself in such a broad scope in the history of humanity and has been incorporated into human consciousness—how subjective and contingent would it be in all its external objectivity if it could not also be grasped in its true objectivity, and thus in the final analysis as a metaphysical truth grounded in the essence of God himself?[6]

Baur conceived of history as a theological discipline grounded in the idea of God's self-mediation, and of theology as a historical discipline committed to the unbiased research of historical science (*Wissenschaft*). Holding these two aspects together proved eventually to be an impossible task because the two disciplines retreated from each other—history into a strictly empirical method, and theology into a confessional stance. Whether the failure was built into the vision, or came about as a result of intellectual and moral weakness, is a question that Hans Frei and I debated and it still engages me today. I had to acknowledge that historical reality is indeed often resistant to rational truth, and that facts have distorted ideals into demonic caricatures, as the twentieth century bears tragic witness.

By keeping at it doggedly, I worked through the complexities of Baur and graduated from Yale with a doctorate in 1963. Along the way I had been introduced to many theologies, from Reinhold Niebuhr and Paul Tillich to Karl Barth; from Richard Niebuhr and Ernst Troeltsch to Schleiermacher, Hegel, and Baur. I wrote my systematic theology "credo" for the Divinity School on Calvin and Tillich. This pairing was an odd combination, but it provided the opportunity to read Calvin's *Institutes*, which I thought I should do as a Presbyterian, and Tillich's *Systematic Theology*. I also read

6. Baur, *Church and Theology in the Nineteenth Century*, 64.

Origen, Augustine, Anselm, Thomas Aquinas, Abelard, and Luther. All these great thinkers made me realize that theology is an inexhaustible topic, more than enough to keep one engaged for a lifetime.

When I arrived at the Divinity School of Vanderbilt University two years later, my vocation as a theologian began. I was immediately exposed to new influences. Ray Hart, my senior colleague in theology, and Robert Funk, a professor of New Testament, were both interested in issues raised by a series called New Frontiers in Theology, edited by James M. Robinson and John B. Cobb Jr. Three volumes were published between 1963 and 1967, each with lengthy introductions by Robinson: *The Later Heidegger and Theology*, with a focal essay by Heinrich Ott (Barth's successor in Basel); *The New Hermeneutic*, with focal essays by Gerhard Ebeling and Ernst Fuchs; and *Theology as History*, with a focal essay by Wolfhart Pannenberg. These were thinkers with which my fairly traditional education at Yale had not acquainted me. I had never read Martin Heidegger and was not familiar with the difference between the early and the late Heidegger. Heidegger did not seem to be a very promising conversation partner for theology because his philosophy was essentially nontheistic. It focused on the "thrownness" of human beings (*Dasein*), the fact that they project themselves into existence as the "there" (*da*) of being (*Sein*). Being is a power or quality, a letting-be, not a thing, and increasingly Heidegger came to understand being in terms of language or linguistic acts. Humans project themselves in response to a primordial "call." This seemed promising to some theologians as a way of interpreting the Word of God and giving it a kind of philosophical underpinning. I read a good bit of Heidegger in my early years at Vanderbilt and tried to appropriate some of his ideas. Gerhard Ebeling, a student of Luther and Bultmann, propounded a "new hermeneutic," which is not just a method but a process in which language itself speaks, a theme set forth in his collection of essays called *Word and Faith* (1963). Wolfhart Pannenberg experienced a conversion to Christianity from a Marxist position and developed a theology of history influenced by Hegel and Barth and oriented to the futurity of events, of which the resurrection of Jesus is the paradigm. Both Ebeling and Pannenberg later published systematic theologies. Jürgen Moltmann, one of Pannenberg's contemporaries, was not featured in the New Frontier series, but he made a major impact with the publication of his *Theology of Hope* (1964), followed by *The Crucified God* (1972) and *The Church in the Power of the Spirit* (1975). He too was influenced by Hegel, Barth, Marxist thought, and the new hermeneutic. In 1967 he joined the Tübingen faculty as a successor to Ebeling, and I heard him lecture there the following year.

All these influences and more contributed to my first attempt at writing theology during my 1968–69 sabbatical in Tübingen: *Jesus—Word and Presence: An Essay in Christology* (published in 1971). This was an attempt, I said, "to move through and beyond interpretations of God's *absence*, of which the death of God theology and the theologies of the future are important recent expressions, to a fresh understanding of his *presence*, definitively so in the words and deeds, death and resurrection, of Jesus of Nazareth." I revealed the influence of Heidegger when I wrote, "Word is an event or a power—the power of the future—that gathers into presence both temporally and spatially, transcending human speech while coming to expression precisely there. As such, word is the event of being itself." Unlike Heidegger, I claimed that this event of being is God or God's Word, and that Jesus was the definitive manifestation of this Word for Christians. This Word lives on in the practice of presence, which constitutes the meaning of the resurrection. My work was not especially original but an amalgam of what I had been reading since 1965.

When I returned to Vanderbilt in the summer of 1969, an essentially new faculty in theology had been appointed. Edward Farley replaced Ray Hart, and Sallie McFague arrived along with Eugene TeSelle. TeSelle taught in the field of ancient and European church history, which he covered with great dexterity, but he also knew quite a bit about modern theology. He was the person to whom you went with questions about specific historical and textual references. Sallie McFague began teaching a few years later and soon became a popular leader in the Divinity School, serving as its first female dean. Her interests shifted from an earlier focus on theology and literature to metaphorical theology, feminist theology, and ecological theology. With books like *Metaphorical Theology* (1982), *Models of God* (1987), and *The Body of God* (1993), McFague became Vanderbilt's best-known theologian, and she attracted excellent students. When she retired in the late 1990s she became a Distinguished Theologian in Residence at the Vancouver School of Theology in British Columbia.

Edward Farley was a challenging conversation partner for me, with a very different set of interests. His first work was on *The Transcendence of God* (1960), which I read in Tübingen when he was being considered for an appointment. He undertook rigorous investigations into the phenomenology of Edmund Husserl and Maurice Merleau-Ponty, and the social world of Alfred Schutz, and their methods shaped his subsequent work. He was a Schleiermacherian rather than a Hegelian. He would often pose issues in terms of opposing positions, tracing the implications of each, and asking which was really meant; whereas my preference was to seek a resolution in a third, mediating position. Because of his learned and sophisticated arguments, he could be quite intimidating. He was five years my senior and I always regarded him with awe but greatly appreciated him as a colleague. The first book he published after coming to Vanderbilt was *Ecclesial Man: A Social Phenomenology of Faith and Reality* (1975), and this was followed by *Ecclesial Reflection: An Anatomy of Theological Method* (1982). Both works were intended as a prolegomenon to theology and focused on such questions as: the ways in which realities are given to theology, how these realities lay claim to truth, how the faith-world is to be described, the role of intersubjectivity in human existence. The second book offered a critique and alternative to the so-called house of authority, which bases its claims on scripture and tradition. Later he applied his method to theological topics such as *Good and Evil* (1990) and *Divine Empathy: A Theology of God* (1996), and he made important theoretical contributions to theological education. The range and depth of his thinking are evident from his interest in "deep symbols," in aesthetics, music, the classics, and politics. These interests are summed up in his memoir, *Thinking About Things and Other Frivolities* (2014). Farley was an original, rigorous thinker, whose ideas I absorbed as much as possible, but I did not follow him.

Vanderbilt Divinity School was able to offer students several quite different theological approaches, which were in friendly conversation with each other for about twenty-five years. We got along well and appreciated each other's work. Included in our group were Jack Forstman, a historian of Christian thought, whose best-known work was *Christian Faith in Dark Times* (1992), and Gene TeSelle, author of *Augustine, the Theologian* (1970) and *Christ in Context* (1975). Both held leadership positions in the Divinity School and their respective churches.

In the early 1970s I became involved in the literature of black theology as the result of teaching a course jointly with Thomas Ogletree and James Lawson, to which I referred earlier. I also began reading Latin American liberation theologians, feminist theologians, and the philosophical theology of Paul Ricoeur. These influences led to a major effort in constructive theology on my part, *New Birth of Freedom: A Theology of Bondage and Liberation* (1976).[7] The first chapter was called "Freedom in America: The Vision, the Fault, the Unfinished Work," picking up on themes from Lincoln's Gettysburg Address. Then I analyzed rival meanings of freedom (political-economic, rational-psychoanalytic, tragic-existential, ecstatic-vitalistic, and pragmatic-technocratic), comparing them with Christian freedom, which I divided into four elements: essential freedom, bound freedom, liberated freedom, and final freedom. My discussion of essential freedom and bound freedom was very much influenced by Ricoeur. Liberated freedom drew upon black and liberation theologies as well as my earlier studies of the New Testament and my engagement with the work of Jürgen Moltmann. I then tried to tie together the struc-

---

7. A forerunner was *Children of Freedom: Black Liberation in Christian Perspective* (1974), to which Gayraud Wilmore wrote a foreword. It was testimony to the impact of James Cone and other black theologians on my outlook.

tures of freedom (autonomy, community, openness) with Jesus' radical freedom (obedience to God, existence for others, personal identity and authority) and a symbolics of freedom (faith, love, life, all consummated in hope, the kingdom of freedom). This was a very ambitious project, and as I look back at it I am astonished by what I was able to accomplish. It provided the foundation for much of my future work, and already I was inclining toward Hegel again, as interpreted by Moltmann and Ricoeur. One reviewer of the work wondered why "the two-edged sword of liberation has to be packed in the cotton balls of . . . German idealism"—but, I responded, the cotton ball really proved to be a cannon ball. Later I described the period in my life from 1968 to 1976 as the loss of innocence and a second theological education. It was that in part because I found myself complicit in the very issues (racism, classism, sexism) I was attempting to ameliorate.

Throughout my career at Vanderbilt I taught Protestant Theology in the Nineteenth Century. We read and discussed Schleiermacher, Hegel, Coleridge, Strauss, Kierkegaard, Bushnell, Harnack, Royce, Troeltsch, and other major figures, including George Eliot and Frederick Douglass. I began desiring a more adequate edition and translation of Hegel's *Lectures on the Philosophy of Religion*, and in the late 1970s made a partial translation of a 1920s version by Georg Lasson, but his edition was inadequate too. I learned about Walter Jaeschke, a scholar at the Hegel Archives, connected with the Ruhr University in Bochum, who had the scholarly expertise and desire to produce a German critical edition. I spent part of a sabbatical in 1980–81 helping with the project.

The original editors of Hegel's *Works* in the 1830s and 1840s amalgamated various manuscripts and auditors' transcriptions into editorially constructed texts. This was especially unfortunate for his lectures on the philosophy of religion, which Hegel delivered four times over an eleven-year period (the summer semesters of 1821, 1824, 1827, and 1831), and which varied each time he presented them. Seemingly incompatible statements appeared alongside each other in the old edition, and the progression in Hegel's understanding of the religions was obscured. The

Part 2: Winter Thoughts

only solution was to present each lecture series as an independent text on its own, but this was more easily said than done. Valuable manuscripts had been lost in the period since Lasson, especially during the Second World War. Hegel's original lecture manuscript of 1821 was preserved in a Berlin library, and reliable transcriptions of his lectures of 1824. But the best sources for 1827 and 1831 were no longer extant. It was possible to reconstruct the lectures of 1827 from the Lasson edition by subtracting from it the passages traceable to 1824. But already in Lasson's time the best sources for the lectures of 1831 were lost, and the only source was an outline of these lectures made by David Friedrich Strauss from notes taken by a student in the summer of 1831. This outline, however, enabled us to identify passages in the *Werke* editions of 1832 and 1840 that were traceable to 1831. In this fashion Jaeschke was able to produce a three-volume critical edition (1983–85) that has proven to be quite successful. Through the Hegel Society of America I found two excellent collaborators: Robert F. Brown of the University of Delaware, and J. Michael Stewart of Farnham, England, a professional translator for UNESCO with an interest in Hegel. Our English translation appeared between 1984 and 1987, and in 1988 we published a one-volume edition containing the lectures of 1827. Brown continued working with Stewart on a critical edition of the *Lectures on the History of Philosophy*; and Stewart and I were collaborating on another project when he died in 1994.

Much of the 1980s was consumed by Hegel, but I was involved in other projects as well. In 1975 the faculty of the Divinity School at Vanderbilt University hosted a group of theologians from major theological schools in the United States to discuss ways in which we could better serve the needs of theological education collaboratively and address specific issues, themes, and problems affecting the church as a whole. The meeting was successful, and we decided to call ourselves the Workgroup on Constructive Theology. With subsequent meetings we made the decision to publish a textbook. The Institute of Cultural and Ecumenical Research in Collegeville, Minnesota, took over sponsorship of the group, and during annual meetings at their conference center we agreed on a format and later discussed draft chapters. Robert H. King and I were designated the coeditors. The book came out in 1982 as *Christian Theology: An Introduction to Its Traditions and Tasks*. A second edition appeared in 1985 with additional chapters,[8] and at the same time a companion volume was published, *Readings in Christian Theology*. For about twenty years these two volumes sold very well and earned enough in royalties to enable the Workgroup to become a self-supporting entity. The Workgroup continues to this day, more than forty years after its founding, having gone through several iterations, new membership, new purposes, and further publications. My own involvement helped to orient my interests and convictions in the 1980s and 1990s.

One such project grew out of a course I had been teaching in the Divinity School and was called *Revisioning the Church: Ecclesial Freedom in the New Paradigm* (1988). This was a short book but it seemed to fill a need because it went through four printings in the next few years. It was very much based on the *Christian Theology* model. The first chapter discussed elements of the church in the classic paradigm: christology and ecclesiology, ecclesia and church, images of ecclesia (people, body, communion, spirit), ecclesia and basileia, marks of the church (one, holy, catholic, apostolic), the Protestant principle (the church visible and invisible), church and sect. The second chapter moved toward a theology of the church in the new paradigm: spirituality and historicality, the church and the praxis of liberation (the black church, Latin American base communities, the feminist ecclesial vision), ecumenism, world

---

8. The book in its final form contained chapters written by David Tracy on Theological Method, Edward Farley and Peter Hodgson on Scripture and Tradition, Langdon Gilkey on God, George Stroup on Revelation, Julian Hartt on Creation and Providence, David Kelsey on Human Being, Robert R. Williams on Sin and Evil, Walter Lowe on Christ and Salvation, Peter Hodgson and Robert C. Williams on the Church, Stephen Sykes on The Sacraments, David Burrell on The Spirit and the Christian Life, Carl Braaten on The Kingdom of God and Life Everlasting, John Cobb on The Religions, and Sallie McFague on The Christian Paradigm. Robert King contributed an Introduction. Each of the chapters considered the doctrine in its classic formulation, the challenges and contributions of modern consciousness, and the "paradigm shifts" required for ongoing discussion in the late twentieth century.

Christianity, and encounter among the religions. The concluding chapter offered a theology of ministry in the new paradigm, and the epilogue reflected on the "ecclesia of freedom."

Another book appeared in 1989 called *God in History: Shapes of Freedom*, this one a more direct consequence of my earlier legacy. It was an attempt at reconstructing a theology of history in light of the challenges of postmodernity. With the collapse of the classic paradigm of "salvation history," according to which God acts directly in special events through a supernatural causality, how can we speak any longer of God's redemptive presence in history? This was an immense challenge, and I took only small steps toward a resolution. I argued that God and history are in some sense correlative realities: God is "in" history, and history is "in" God. To say that God is in history means that God is an efficacious power of transformation for the good, interacting with all the other factors in history, not compelling or coercing but persuading and inviting, shaping scenes of freedom in the midst of oppression and bondage. The paradigmatic shape of freedom is the figure of Christ, who proclaims the in-breaking of God's "project" (*basileia*) and suffers the inevitable consequences. The Christian vision is tragicomic because it is oriented toward redemption but includes suffering and death. To say that history is in God means that history, like nature, belongs to the divine milieu; history is not simply a network of autonomous and contingent actions but is directed to a purpose, which is to glorify God and promote human and cosmic flourishing. Do assertions like this require a colossal leap of faith, or are they guided by what is actually going on in history? My conversation partners in this book included not only Hegel and Baur but also Ernst Troeltsch, Paul Ricoeur, process theology, and liberation theology.

These and other ideas were incorporated into a book based on lectures for an introductory course in theology: *Winds of the Spirit: A Constructive Christian Theology* (1994). It was my own modest *summa theologica*, and for a few years it had an impact. The book is divided into three main parts: interpreting, contextualizing, and revisioning. Interpreting discusses methodological questions, such as what it means to think theologically, the resources and dimensions of theology, and the task of construction in a deconstructive age. Contextualizing describes three quests characteristic of postmodernity: the emancipatory quest, the ecological quest, and the dialogical quest. Revisioning argues that theology must be reconstructed in conversation with these quests. The emancipatory quest points toward the freedom of God; the ecological quest toward the love of God; and the dialogical quest toward the oneness/wholeness of God. These together constitute a kind of trinity: God is the one who loves in freedom, a formula indebted to Karl Barth. God is the One (Creator, Abba); God is in the world (creation, nature, human being, love, Christ incarnate); and God is Spirit (Christ risen, the liberation of the world, the perfection of God). Philosophically expressed, God is identity, difference, and mediation.

The title metaphor, "Winds of the Spirit," derives from my sailing experience.

> Theology [I wrote] is rather like sailing. It is in contact with powerful, fluid elements, symbolized by wind and water, over which it has little control and by which it is drawn and driven toward mysterious goals. The ship of theology has no foundation other than itself, no external prop, but only the structural integrity and interplay of its component parts, which enable it to float and sail. Occasionally the ship has to be taken into port for repairs and refitting. On the open water sailing can be an exhilarating and joyous adventure but also one filled with danger and disappointment. Truth, value, and beauty do not exist in the abstract but are created in the act of sailing through a symbiosis of ship and elemental forces.[9]

For over thirty years I owned a Javelin day sailor, which I sailed on Percy Priest Lake near Nashville. Initially my son or daughter, and occasionally my wife, went with me, but in later years students from the Divinity School and Graduate Department of Religion were my crewmates. Sailing proved to be a wonderful way to relax

9. *Winds of the Spirit*, 3.

with students: we had a lot of fun, hilarious incidents occurred, and many close friendships were formed. After I retired, the supply of students dwindled and eventually ran out. But I still have a Sunfish in Eagles Mere, which I sail during the summer. On a windy day, the Sunfish is as fun as any boat.

As I look back on my work during the seventies, eighties, and nineties, I have two primary reactions. First, the work is duplicative more than it is original. By duplicative I mean that it incorporates ideas and influences that were present at the time of writing—starting, for example, with the new hermeneutic, then moving on to the black, liberation, and feminist theologies, the ecological and dialogical theologies, the idea of a new paradigm in theological construction, and the need for contextualization. I did not break any new frontiers of my own but reflected and synthesized what was going on. My second reaction is that broadly visionary works such as *Winds of the Spirit* are not in vogue today. This is a darker, more pessimistic era. Theology has become balkanized, split into various factions and interests, each pursuing its own agenda, generally tolerant of but not especially interested in what others are doing. For the most part, conflicts and differences are accepted as a de facto reality, and visions are passé. Great figures such as those found in the nineteenth and twentieth centuries have not yet made an appearance in the twenty-first century. Around the turn of the twenty-first century, I realized that my efforts in constructive theology had come to an end. I had said what I had to say, and it was time to move on. Most of my books had grown out of courses and seminars that I had taught over the years. It has been said that good teachers bring their students to the frontiers of their own thinking and face to face with open questions. I hope this is true, but at least it provided a rationale for doing what I was doing, trying to integrate teaching and writing.

In 2001 a book came out that indicated a new direction. It was called *The Mystery Beneath the Real: Theology in the Fiction of George Eliot*. I had become interested in the writings of George Eliot (the pseudonym of Mary Ann Evans, 1819–80) through nineteenth-century studies, and over several summers I read her novels. She clearly had religious interests, starting from her early evangelicalism and moving through her later religion of humanity toward something more interesting, a "religion of the future." I summarized:

> This would be a truthful religion without accusation and consolation, a practical religion oriented to human feelings, needs and deeds, a spiritual religion attuned to the mystery beneath the real, and a religion open to the idea of a sympathetic, suffering, (omni)present God. She lacked the categories to articulate the theological aspects of this religion very clearly. What she needed was an understanding of a God-in-process, a God who does not control the course of world events but interacts with them, becoming God through a process of self-divestment and self-reunion, a fellow-sufferer who empowers humans through a kind of sympathetic presence, a God who both preserves and transforms all things within the divine life.[10]

I was connecting my own interest in such a God with the realities that come forth in George Eliot's fictional world. Her Madonna-like heroines seem to mediate processes of redemptive transformation: Janet Dempster in *Scenes of Clerical Life*, Dinah Morris in *Adam Bede*, Maggie Tulliver in *The Mill on the Floss*, Romola in the novel named for her, Dorothea Brooke in *Middlemarch*. Men play this role too in *Scenes of Clerical Life*, *Silas Marner*, *Felix Holt*, and *Daniel Deronda*. In George Eliot's description of the ordinary, something extraordinary sometimes shines through. Faith and especially love—the mystery beneath the real—have a quality of "superabundance," which is not bound by the logic of normal human relations, but is present in and through them. The image of superabundance is mentioned in "Janet's Repentance," one of the *Scenes of Clerical Life*, and refers not only to a garden (a paradise) but also to the superabundance of Edgar Tryan's ministry, which brought about Janet's repentance. *Middlemarch* ends with these words: "The growing good of the world is partly dependent

---

10. *The Mystery Beneath the Real*, 13–14.

on unhistoric acts; and that things are not so ill with you and me as they might have been, is half-owing to the number who lived faithfully a hidden life, and rest in unvisited tombs." My observation is that these words "tell us more about God's real presence in the world than all the sermons of glory and triumph, all the naïve belief in divine providence and protection."[11] This was my own testament as well as George Eliot's, and her novels could express it as well if not better than any theology could. Theology itself, I had learned from Edward Farley, is a kind of fiction. It creates imaginative variations on what history offers as real in a quest for the mystery beneath the real.

This might have been a useful idea to pursue further, but I lacked expertise in literary criticism and broader knowledge of literary figures, so I returned to a more familiar topic. I had taught seminars on Hegel's philosophy of religion and had accumulated a good deal of material, which I put into a book: *Hegel and Christian Theology: A Reading of the Lectures on the Philosophy of Religion* (2005). A close study of the critical edition of the *Lectures* that I had helped produce in the 1980s had not yet been published, so that is what I provided. I viewed Hegel as offering a speculative reconstruction of Christian theology that should be as fruitful a source for contemporary theological reflection as the works of Schleiermacher and Kierkegaard, Barth and Tillich, Whitehead and Ricoeur. Since then others have taken this theological interpretation further, notably Robert R. Williams in *Tragedy, Recognition, and the Death of God* (2012) and *Hegel on the Proofs and the Personhood of God* (2017). But the universe of aficionados of Hegel's religious thought is not large. As Williams points out, Hegel is too theological for the philosophers and too philosophical for the theologians. Williams is another of my friends who has passed away recently.

In 2003 I retired from Vanderbilt and began looking around for projects to keep me busy. Having emptied my own font of ideas, I thought the most useful thing I could provide would be translations of works of recognized importance. Fortunately Robert F.

11. Ibid., 120. On the aspect of "superabundance," see 39–40.

Brown, with whom I had collaborated in the 1980s, was interested in doing the same. Brown has a fine gift for translation, and collaborating with him would produce better results than working on my own. Oxford University Press was willing to take over and continue the Hegel Lectures Series initiated in the 1980s. Brown had begun a translation of a critical edition of the *Lectures on the History of Philosophy* in the early nineties but because of a change in publishers was able to complete the three volumes only some fifteen years later. He also undertook a translation of the Hotho transcription of the *Lectures on the Philosophy of Art*. In 2009 I published a new translation of *Hegel's Lectures on the Proofs of the Existence of God*, which made this nearly forgotten work accessible. Robert Williams contributed a translation of Hegel's *Lectures on the Philosophy of Spirit*. These correspond to the first division of the third part of Hegel's *Encyclopedia of the Philosophical Sciences*, and constitute the philosophy of subjective spirit (anthropology, phenomenology of spirit, psychology), as compared with the philosophy of objective spirit, the second division of the third part (the topic of a separate book, *The Philosophy of* Right), and the philosophy of absolute spirit, the third division (Hegel's absolute spirit is absolving, intrinsically relational spirit, and appears as art, religion, and philosophy).

Brown and I collaborated on a new edition of Hegel's *Lectures on the Philosophy of World History*, which came out in 2011. We combined Hegel's own manuscripts of the Introduction from 1822, 1828, and 1830–31, which had been published by Walter Jaeschke in a volume of the *Gesammelte Werke* (1995), and a transcription of the lectures of 1822–23 by Hotho and Griesheim, published by Ilting, Brehmer, and Seelmann in the Hegel *Vorlesungen* series (1996). This edition cleared up many of the textual questions left over from earlier editions of the *Weltgeschichte*, which had combined materials from different lecture series into an editorially constructed text. We are awaiting the critical edition of Karl Hegel's transcription of the lectures of 1830–31, and selections of materials from intervening years, to complete the project in a second volume.

Part 2: Winter Thoughts

I wrote a book about the first volume in 2012 called *Shapes of Freedom: Hegel's Philosophy of World History in Theological Perspective*. I revisited issues I had first addressed in *God and History*, but now with a better grasp of Hegel: especially his view of history as the progress of the consciousness of freedom, his argument that human passions and divine ideas are "woven" together to form the fabric of history, his understanding of how freedom is actualized in the state, his incorporation of the tragic into the divine life, and his construction of the course of world history as it moves through four "worlds": Oriental (one is free), Greek and Roman (some are free), and European-modern (all are free). Such a view may be too theological for most historians and philosophers, but I think it offers untapped resources for theologians who want to understand how God is efficaciously present in history without rupturing history. Unfortunately, not many theologians are willing to engage this question—which seems to me to be the overriding theological question of our time—in a serious way. One of the few exceptions is John Cobb, for whom Whitehead's process philosophy offers a route to an answer similar to what I think is provided by Hegel. For both philosophers, God is an "ideal" factor in history, a factor that does not coerce and compel but rather guides and persuades. For the ideal to become real in concrete circumstances, human action is required, which, being imperfect, leads to tragic conflicts and defeats as well as partial and always ambiguous accomplishments. History has a goal or trajectory, the actualization of freedom in human life—which is but an obscure image of the perfect freedom of the divine life. This goal is achieved, not through a steady advance, but through epochal cultural shifts, which produce retrograde moments as well as new insights into the meaning of freedom and the purpose of life.

With the completion of the Hegel projects, Brown and I turned to two of the many books by Baur that remained untranslated. I had made an initial effort with his *Lehrbuch der christlichen Dogmengeschichte* in 2003, but the results were unsatisfactory and I put the work aside. However, Brown was able to revise what I had done, creating a much more accurate and readable version.

Our joint translation was published in 2014 by Oxford University Press as *History of Christian Dogma*. This is actually a "textbook" that Baur himself created from his lectures on the history of Christian dogma, which, when published posthumously by his son (1865–67), ran to four volumes and 2,300 pages. The textbook is less than 400 pages in the second edition of 1858. It contains an important introduction that discusses the object and method of the history of dogma, and the relationship of the history of dogma to church history, dogmatics, and the history of philosophy. For Christian faith, dogma or doctrine is not Christian teaching "in its original and still indeterminate sense as *logos theou*, word of God, but rather already in a specific wording or formulation, in respect to which the undeniable human aspect of the form must be distinguished from the divine content subsisting in itself."[12] This tension between content and form is a decisive factor throughout the history of dogma. On the one hand, dogma contains what is divine and absolute, but, on the other hand, it contains this truth only in human form, and these forms are constantly shifting and multiplying. The method of the history of dogma is to follow the movement of dogma itself, but this always entails an engagement with human consciousness and subjectivity. The history of dogma continues into our own time rather than terminating with the Reformation, as others (such as Harnack) have claimed. Baur treats this history in three major periods. (1) From the apostolic age to the end of the sixth century: the dogma of the ancient church, or the substantiality of dogma. (2) From the beginning of the seventh century to the Reformation: the dogma of the Middle Ages, or the dogma of inwardly reflected consciousness. (3) From the Reformation to the most recent times: dogma in the modern era, or dogma and free self-consciousness. Thus the chief forms in the history of dogma are substance (objective doctrine), inward reflection, and free self-consciousness. Free self-consciousness means that the objectivity of dogma and the subjectivity of consciousness are unified, but always for a particular time and place.

---

12. Baur, *History of Christian Dogma*, 49.

Part 2: Winter Thoughts

Baur also lectured on New Testament theology, and his son published these lectures in 1864. Brown translated this work as *Lectures on New Testament Theology*, which appeared from Oxford in 2016. Here Baur addresses Christian teaching "in its original and still indeterminate sense" in the form of the teaching of Jesus, which he summarizes as follows:

> Christianity appeared foremost as a strengthening of moral consciousness, as a moral power that sought to arouse in human beings the awareness of their moral self-determination, the energy of their own moral freedom and autonomy. This moral element makes itself known in the simplest statements of the Sermon on the Mount, as the purest and clearest content of Jesus' teaching. In fact it is the substantial core of Christianity, and all else, howsoever great its significance may be, stands in a more or less secondary and incidental relationship to this moral element. It is the foundation on which everything else first can be built. Even though it hardly has the form and the complexion of what Christianity became historically, it nevertheless already is implicitly the whole of Christianity. All too soon it was able to be suppressed by the dogmatism developing from Christian consciousness, to be set in its shadow, to be overlaid and stifled. . . . Yet this moral element ever remains the firmly unshakable point to which people always had to return once again.[13]

With the death of Jesus the focus shifts from Jesus' teaching to his person, its absolute significance and saving work. This conviction was attained by the Apostle Paul, who discovered in Jesus' death not defeat but victory, the realization of righteousness in a way that could not be attained by fulfilling the law: the destiny of the messiah is to die for others, not to reign on earth. Paul was the first and the greatest of the apostles, but he was followed by others, who authored the various writings of the New Testament, each with its specific theological framework and social milieu. Baur emphasizes

---

13. Baur, *Lectures on New Testament Theology*, 108.

not the unity but the diversity of the New Testament, which constitutes the initial phase in the history of theological reflection.

Following these two primary texts, Brown and I translated a recent collection of essays called *Ferdinand Christian Baur and the History of Early Christianity*, edited by Martin Bauspiess, Christof Landmesser, and David Lincicum (Oxford, 2017), the first significant work on Baur to appear in English for many years. This collection was originally published in Germany in 2014 and contains ten chapters written in German and five in English. The authors discuss Baur's relation to Strauss, Möhler, and Hegel, his historical and exegetical perspectives, and his influences. They argue for Baur's relevance to contemporary methodological discussions and his ongoing historical significance.

These translations provide a way of keeping two senior citizens occupied, and we intend to continue as long as possible. Presently we are working on the first and last volumes of Baur's five-volume history of the Christian Church: *Christianity and the Christian Church of the First Three Centuries*, and *Church and Theology in the Nineteenth Century*. These books will appear from Cascade Books in Eugene, Oregon.

∼

Thus far I have discussed "theologies" in terms of theologians who have influenced me and my own contributions to the discipline. I will attempt to draw some conclusions from what I have written and offer some judgments about outstanding issues for today. I focus on three factors: realism, idealism, and their confluence in the construction of history.

Theology is a kind of fiction that offers imaginative variations on what is real. But first it must attend to the real, with all the detailed descriptions of the novelist, all the nuances in human attitudes, feelings, and actions, all the ambiguities and tragic failures that characterize human communities. Many theologians and preachers today avoid the real: they offer escapes and fantasies rather than honest engagement with the material world and

Part 2: Winter Thoughts

human culture. The tendency toward supernaturalism and the miraculous is the clearest evidence of this escape, and the interest in the miraculous has not diminished over the ages on the part of many religious people. The problem is that many more people do not find such a worldview persuasive any longer, and they have withdrawn from engagement with religion. They are living in a secular, scientific world, and their values are determined accordingly. These are the values of quantitative measurement, pleasure, and altruism. Pleasure is provided by internet and phone devices, material success, sexual activities, games and music, alcohol and drugs. Altruism arises from the recognition that cooperation is often more beneficial than competition. This is the reality most people live in today, but theology and the church are disconnected from it and offer an alternative world that in many ways is less real. Life in fact is hard, a long and often discouraging struggle with relentless forces—the forces of nature; of the human body with its vulnerability to illness, disease, and aging; of the human psyche with its emotions, aggressions, and depressions. Even though the level of large-scale violence has declined when measured over centuries, there is still plenty of it around and it assumes new forms, such as holocausts, terror attacks, gun violence, religious and fanatical hatreds, the ever-present threat of nuclear war. Poverty is widespread throughout the world, including the United States, where the gap between poverty and wealth widens because of political and economic policies. The coming global environmental crisis may render all previous world crises trivial by comparison.

These are the realities with which theology should be engaged. Instead it is often forced to deal with petty questions such as those about sexual orientation and abortion—questions that should have been settled long ago and that should not continue to dominate the public forum. Prejudices about sexual orientation are rooted in ancient and still powerful stereotypes. The notion that a human person exists from the moment of conception is not persuasive, and it distracts from policies supporting human well-being after birth (such as education, health, adequate income). The quality of life is crucial, not simply the sheer existence of it. The belief that God intervenes in history to save people in miraculous ways is equally non-persuasive. If God can do this in some instances (those that serve our interests), why should God not always intervene to prevent the vast suffering that is everywhere present, to cancel the great tragedies of history, to protect the environment from the damage that civilization is inflicting on it? God is not a magician who controls what goes on in the world, although many people seem to think of God that way. Christ is not a divine savior who dies a substitutionary death and frees us from responsibility for our deeds. Naïve ideas about God and Christ account for the irrelevance of religion in the world. Theology does not seem much interested in the hard task of reconstructing conceptions of God and Christ in ways that take into account the realities of life as we actually experience them. These realities offer resources for theology if it is open to receiving them: the emancipatory struggles of oppressed peoples, the heightened consciousness of feminism and gender differences, the pluralism of religious and cultural traditions, the participation of humans in a vast ecological system that can be thrown out of balance all too easily.

Theology offers imaginative variations on these realities. This is where ideality comes into play. God is the supreme ideality: pure spirit and absolute rationality. God is the source of creative possibility, imagination, novelty, and purpose. God is not a being among beings, a material entity or natural force. God lacks physicality and cannot be measured, weighed, or utilized like a material object. God is an idea—certainly a human idea, but also an objectively self-actualizing and self-sustaining idea. Without ideality, the universe would be an immense, soulless interaction of meaningless natural forces. God's ideality includes values that we associate with goodness, love, freedom, trustworthiness, community, superabundance. This ideality goes forth from itself and creates an other than itself, the material and spiritual world, which has its own powers and autonomies that often go awry and conflict with each other, producing tragic and destructive consequences. What we call "spirit" is the ideal embodied in the material and human world. God is absolute spirit, which means that God overreaches and embraces the world of finite spirits within godself, related to all that is not-God.

We do not know the ideal in and for itself except in a purely abstract, rational sense. The advance from Kant to Hegel in the history of philosophy is the advance from abstract rationality to concrete historicality. Hegel says that history is constructed from the interweaving of the divine idea and human passions, and that history is the progress of the consciousness of freedom. The idea provides values and direction; the passions provide energy and movement. History has meaning, but also struggle and conflict. Just how God as the absolute idea provides values and direction to history is one of the most difficult theological questions—the question of how God acts efficaciously in history without rupturing historical processes. Hegel and Whitehead point to the same answer, namely, that the divine values and guidance function as a lure, a pattern, an invitation calling for a human response. Without the response, without the determination to shape history in accord with the divine pattern, there is no efficacious presence of God in history. *We* are the agents of the divine purpose, but very often we confuse our own purposes with the ideal purpose. We need a concrete paradigm, and Christians believe that Jesus Christ is this paradigm. He is a human being who is filled by the Spirit of God and becomes an agent of God's work in the world through his teaching and example, and his death on a cross. He is not the only such agent. Other religions and cultures have their own paradigmatic agents, such as Moses, Muhammad, Brahman, the Buddha, and among these agents there seems to be a broad concurrence about good and evil, which is not to deny their very real differences. History has produced other great figures who provide moral and intellectual guidance, from Socrates and Plato to Dietrich Bonhoeffer and Martin Luther King Jr. They all represent incarnations of the divine idea, and they all contribute to the progress of the consciousness of freedom. This progression is never complete because history is a mixture of comedy and tragedy, of freedom and oppression, of good and evil. The death of God on the cross of Christ signifies that tragedy is taken up into the divine life and negated there; it continues as a negated element, and this negation gives Christians the courage to face the tragic conflicts of history. Christ, therefore, is for Christians the normative paradigm of God in history.

Christian theology today seems to be mostly confessional and evangelical theology. Confessional theologies attempt to promote the distinctive trajectory of the great confessions—Catholic, Orthodox, Lutheran, Reformed, Anglican, Wesleyan, sectarian. Evangelical theologies are committed to the infallibility of scripture, which they often construe in very literal terms and on the basis of their own unacknowledged prejudices. The possibility of a plurality and conflict of interpretations is not recognized. As an alternative to confessional and evangelical approaches, I propose a critical revisionist theology. Such a theology is critical because it recognizes that the whole of the biblical and doctrinal tradition must be scrutinized by thought. It is revisionist because it believes traditional formulations must be re-conceptualized in light of the challenges of modern culture. The issues of importance today—ecological, emancipatory, and dialogical—are not illuminated by confessional differences and literal readings of the Bible. These issues demand hard, original, and adventurous thought. Such was the agenda adopted over forty years ago by the Workgroup on Constructive Theology. The Workgroup continues its labors today with a new generation of scholars and teachers. I wish them and others who share their vision Godspeed.

Ernst Troeltsch, one of the forerunners of revisionist theology, said that cynicism about the future is the danger of those who become too familiar with the hypocrisy, mendacity, and opportunism of the present. He struggled to maintain an attitude of hopeful realism in the aftermath of the First World War. We too must struggle to maintain such an attitude in face of the collapse of the liberal consensus in politics that guided Western democracies since the Second World War.

13

Politics

My thoughts about politics are random and scattered, shaped by old memories, recent events, and diverse sources. Eva and I grew up in Republican families, but we switched allegiances while in college. We proudly voted for John Kennedy in 1960. When we arrived in Nashville five years later, Tennessee was still reliably Democratic—not liberal Democratic but southern Democratic, with a heritage of racism and an appeal to rural as well as urban areas. Tennessee had been a one-party state since the Civil War,[1] and this party in its declining years produced some fine senators, including Estes Kefauver, Albert Gore Sr., Al Gore Jr., and Jim Sasser. But changes were underway. A long-term reaction was setting in to the civil rights activism of the national Democratic Party in the 1960s. Albert Gore Sr. lost his seat to candy-family heir Bill Brock in 1970,[2] and that was a sign of changes to come.

---

1. Some of the early and most decisive battles of the Civil War were fought in Tennessee, such as Fort Donelson and Shiloh. This tragically bloody conflict shaped Southern history for at least the next hundred years, and its aftermath is still felt today as neo-Confederates assert themselves anew. The Democratic Party became the party of Southern whites during Reconstruction and Jim Crow. The magnitude of Southern resistance following the War is underscored by Ron Chernow's brilliant biography *Grant*.

2. Vanderbilt Divinity School declared a reading week just prior to the

Over a period of about twenty-five years, Tennessee swung all the way around to become a different kind of one-party state. The Tennessee Republican Party is not an extreme right-wing party, and it has produced two conservative Republican senators, Lamar Alexander and Bob Corker.[3] But it represents a reaction to social and political liberalism, and in 2016 Tennessee provided one of the largest margins of support for Donald Trump. Pennsylvania has undergone a similar change, but not as extreme. Its rural areas have moved to the right, but its two large metropolitan centers have made it a swing state in recent years. It along with Michigan and Minnesota gave Trump his narrow electoral victory in 2016. One of the ironies of Eva's and my existence is that in the winter we live in a progressive city in a conservative state, and in the summer we live in a conservative county in a (moderately) progressive state.

It is the decline of the liberal democratic consensus in American politics that concerns me as much as the election of Trump. "'Liberal' has long been a dirty word to the American political right," says First Words columnist Nikil Saval.[4] It should not be a dirty word to the right, any more than "conservative" should be a dirty word to the political left. That it has become so reflects the coarsening and cynicism of political discourse. Many books have been written about the decline of liberalism.[5] Explanations have to do with economic and cultural shifts that have led to the weakening of the middle class, disdain for what is regarded as liberal "elitism," the breakdown of trust in public institutions, and the shift to

---

election, and pretty much the entire student body and faculty turned out to campaign for Gore. Such a thing could not happen today.

3. As conservative Republicans, Alexander and Corker voted to deny Barack Obama his Supreme Court nomination and to dismantle the Affordable Care Act. In this respect their position was no different than that of the right wing. But Alexander tried to salvage reimbursements to health insurance companies for two years, and when Corker decided not to run again, he spoke the truth about Trump. Both senators ultimately supported the Republican tax bill, which rewards the donor class, cuts services, and increases the deficit.

4. *The New York Times Magazine*, July 9, 2017, 11.

5. One of the most recent is Luce, *The Retreat of Western Liberalism*.

a hard-right agenda that does not tolerate nuance and restraint. These changes did not happen just by accident or as the result of liberalism's failure. According to a new book by Nancy MacLean,[6] right-wing theorists have argued that all interest groups push for their own agenda rather than the public good. In a democracy, the majority of voters demand an investment in public services paid for by taxing wealth. To prevent this from happening, the alternative is a form of oligarchy or despotism controlled by wealthy elites in their own interest. A "stealth" agenda is required to undermine trust in public institutions and to get the public to direct its anger at these institutions—at liberal democracy in general—and away from increasing income and wealth inequality. This cynical agenda, first formulated by James Buchanan, has been bought and paid for by Charles and David Koch, and it has been enormously successful.

It has brought a breakdown in a consensus that goes back to the Enlightenment of the eighteenth and nineteenth centuries, a consensus that affirmed human dignity, equality, rights, freedom, and reason. The Enlightenment broke the grip of authoritarian systems, but it was itself incomplete, being the product mostly of an educated and privileged class. The struggles during the twentieth century and beyond on the part of women, African Americans, gays and lesbians, the poor, and other marginalized groups for their own rights and recognition should be viewed as a continuation of the Enlightenment project. These struggles, especially as they have manifested themselves recently in immigration from impoverished or war-torn countries, have triggered a backlash among those wanting to maintain their sense of ethnic identity and cultural/religious superiority. Trump's election has emboldened openly hard-right groups to express their hatred of liberalism in all its forms. These groups bring arrogance, violence, and irrationality to bear against restraint, nonviolence, and reason. Once

---

6. *Democracy in Chains*. This book provides a chilling account of how today's right-wing theories originated in Virginia in the 1950s as part of a strategy to resist school integration.

this process has begun, it is hard to reverse; the next step beyond despotism is fascism.[7]

Perhaps a clash in moral-religious worldviews underlies the decline in the liberal democratic consensus. David Brooks suggests as much when he writes[8] that "the profound equality of every individual was an idea that flowed directly from the Hebrew Bible. The story Americans told about themselves was a biblical story— an exodus story of various diverse peoples leaving oppression, crossing a wilderness and joining together to help create a promised land." But the Trump-Bannon creed is "anti-biblical." "It's a zero-sum struggle of class and ethnic conflict. The traits Trump embodies are narcissism, not humility; combativeness, not love; the sanctification of the rich and blindness toward the poor."

The biblical worldview has a fundamental liberality and rationality about it. Hegel argued long ago that faith is a form of knowledge that should not be threatened by critical thinking, and that reason has its ground in the ultimate rationality of things, for which the religious name is God. As "absolute," God is unconditional meaning, truth, and liberality. As finite beings we know this truth only in part, but we *must* seek to know it, and it makes itself known in our seeking. I spent my entire career attempting to articulate a form of theological liberalism that represents a critical engagement with religious truth. In its Christian form this liberalism affirms the centrality of sin and redemption, of Christ and the Holy Spirit. It learns from the great cloud of witnesses through the ages, but it faces new challenges and must find its own formulations. It

---

7. Volker Ullrich documents how fascism gradually, at first almost imperceptibly, took hold in the most enlightened nation in Europe, Germany, after the First World War, in *Hitler: Ascent* 1889–1939. The underlying economic and cultural conditions in the United States today are different from those in Germany a hundred years ago, but our nation is dangerously polarized politically, and those with extreme views (racist and fascist) have increased as a proportion of the population (witness Charlottesville). Fortunately Trump does not (yet) match the rhetorical and demagogic skills of Hitler, and democratic voices have been free (so far) to express their opposition and block part of Trump's agenda, thanks to our balance of powers.

8. Op-ed in *The New York Times*, October 27, 2017.

recognizes ambiguity, conflict, confusion, and tragedy in human affairs, but its own vision is tragicomic.

Maintaining the comic aspect of this vision in an age that feels mostly tragic is challenging, to say the least. It does not mean being naïve about differences. It does not mean demonizing genuine conservatism—although of course we must condemn racist and fascist ideologies, zero-sum struggles, and stealth agendas. We need to understand what drives people away from a common vision of human flourishing, and invite them to share this vision, to look beyond immediate self-interest to precisely a greater public good. Loyalty to the commonwealth of God demands no less.

Such a view is reinforced by reading Suzy Hansen's *Notes on a Foreign Country: An American in a Post-American World*. This book is written from the perspective of an expat living in Turkey and seeing her own country through a very different lens. Her own originally naïve views were shattered by the realization that the United States is often not admired by foreigners, and that it is regarded as an imperial power attempting to impose its own economic and political agenda on the rest of the world. Thanks to the influence of James Baldwin in particular, she sees American history as deeply shadowed by the legacy of slavery and racism, which the U.S. has projected outward in its antipathy toward Middle Eastern and Asian culture in general and Islam in particular. The American reaction to 9/11 has had a damaging impact, creating fears and stereotypes, and weakening our influence among democratic nations. American innocence in believing that the United States is the greatest and most exceptional nation in the world has not died out, despite Watergate, Vietnam, the failures in foreign policy, the growth in gun violence, the decline in material conditions, and the increasing disparity between wealth and poverty.

Hansen writes at the end: "The possibility of redemption is not because of our own God-given beneficence but proof of the world's unending generosity."[9] If the world is generous, is it because God is generous?

This question leads me back to Hegel's *Lectures on the Philosophy of World History* and the question as to whether and how God is redemptively present in the world. I will attempt to elaborate my views a little more fully in these concluding paragraphs. In *Shapes of Freedom*[10] I describe how for Hegel the divine idea and human passions "form the weft and the warp in the fabric that world history spreads before us." The term translated as "weft" means literally a "driving" or "striking," and is related to the "pulse" or "stroke" of a shuttle. This is an image that Hegel associates with the idea, which drives back and forth across the "warp" of human passions, weaving the fabric of history, which gradually assumes the pattern of "ethical freedom."[11] The idea is elsewhere described as a "counterstroke" that reverses the transition from finite to infinite into a transition from infinite to finite. History is a divine-human production in which the idea furnishes the guiding propulsive power and the passions the material substrate. Such a view is very unfashionable today among historians and theologians, but I think it offers insight into how God's presence in history occurs without rupturing the fabric of history.

Another famous metaphor introduced by Hegel into the *Philosophy of World History* is that of the "cunning of reason."[12] I interpret it as follows: reason, because it is *spiritual* and not physical or natural power, must work *negatively*; it overcomes opposition and evil not directly, not by intervention in natural processes or by supernatural means, but indirectly, by letting evil combat

---

9. Hansen, *Notes on a Foreign Country*, 247.

10. *Shapes of Freedom*, especially chaps. 2 and 5. These concluding thoughts are found in a somewhat different form in an article I have written, "Hegel on the Proofs, Personhood, and Freedom of God," for *The Owl of Minerva*. They seem relevant to a theological view of politics.

11. Hegel, *Lectures on the Philosophy of World History*, 1:147.

12. Ibid., 96.

evil, allowing passions to wear themselves out, using instruments against their own purposes. Reason in its "cunning" subverts human intentions, has the power of apparent weakness (not of force or violence), and brings good out of evil. The deep tragedy of history is that in the process many are sacrificed and a terrible price is paid for human freedom. But the vision is ultimately tragicomic, for good *does* come out of evil, however imperfectly, and reconciliation *is* accomplished through conflict. Because cunning has the power of apparent weakness, the metaphor can be stretched further to suggest that the power of cunning is like the power of the cross, where God in human shape dies at the hands of human violence but where God's purpose prevails nonetheless. God "lets" human beings do as they please, but God's will prevails. The cross represents the great reversal, the counterthrust of the idea. God does not cause or desire the tortured death of a human being, but draws out its unintended consequences. It is true that Hegel says, when speaking of Alexander the Great, that "one must be prepared for blood and strife when one turns to world history, for they are the means by which the world spirit drives itself forward." But he also says, when speaking of the Trojan War, that the suffering and devastation of war represent a gigantic exercise in "futility," which can only be described as tragic and makes of history a "slaughterhouse."[13] Human beings gradually learn from their mistakes; their passions are disciplined by the world spirit. Today we are no longer prepared for blood and strife: they must be driven as far out of history as possible.

The cunning of reason represents the negative work of the idea, but there is also a positive work in which the idea no longer appears as a *counterthrust* but a *lure*. Morality, ethical life, the state, art, and religion are means that are suitable to their ends because they are governed by the divine principle of reason, the divine idea of freedom. Hegel says that human beings, in fulfilling rational ends, not only fulfill their own particular ends but also "*participate* in that rational end itself, and are thereby ends in themselves."[14]

13. Ibid., 421, 359, 90.
14. Ibid., 97.

The term "participation" suggests that the divine idea functions as a "lure" that draws human actions to higher ends; it has the power of "persuasion," not coercion (and not simply that of cunning). Hegel does not develop this theme very fully or clearly, but it is picked up a century later in process philosophy.

There is for Hegel a deep sense in which history and politics themselves provide a proof of God's redemptive presence. He makes the extraordinary claim that "reason governs the world" and that therefore "world history is a rational process." The religious form of this conviction is that "the world is not given over to chance and external, contingent causes, but is *ruled by providence*." "Divine providence is the wisdom that has the infinite power to actualize its purposes, that is, the absolute, rational, final purpose of the world." History, he says, is "the progress of the consciousness of freedom," a consciousness that slowly develops through diverse cultures over a period of three thousand years. Hegel holds to this conviction despite the fact that history is also a "slaughterhouse in which the happiness of peoples, the wisdom of states, and the virtues of individuals are sacrificed."[15] You have to read the *Lectures on the Philosophy of World History* to learn how Hegel reconciles these factors. From our perspective today, his resolution is no longer satisfactory to the extent that he regards large-scale violence as an inevitable fact, but he is moving in the right direction.

Similar views were expressed by Dietrich Bonhoeffer in a famous passage, written at the beginning of 1943, a passage that simply expresses the heart of Christian faith:

> I believe that God both can and will bring good out of evil. For that purpose he needs people who make the best use of everything. I believe God will give us all the power we need to resist in all times of distress. . . . I believe that even our errors and mistakes are turned to good account. . . . I believe God is not just timeless fate, but that he waits upon and answers sincere prayer and responsible action.[16]

---

15. Ibid., 79, 83 (italics original), 88, 90.
16. Bonhoeffer, *Prisoner for God*, 21. Bonhoeffer was arrested on April 5,

Part 2: Winter Thoughts

If history could be viewed as a slaughterhouse early in the nineteenth century, how much more so at the beginning of the twenty-first century! Yet the scale of human violence is clearly declining in proportion to population, according to a remarkable book by Steven Pinker. This claim may seem counter-factual in light of two devastating world wars in the twentieth century, but on the long scale of history it is true. All the measures of violence are down, especially since the Enlightenment. Pinker, a social scientist, identifies five historical forces that explain this downward trend. There is nothing explicitly religious about these forces, but we could well view them as evidences of providence. I quote at length:

> The *Leviathon*, a state and judiciary with a monopoly on the legitimate use of force, can defuse the temptation of exploitative attack, inhibit the impulse for revenge, and circumvent the self-serving biases that make all parties believe they are on the side of the angels. *Commerce* is a positive-sum game in which everybody can win; as technological progress allows the exchange of goods and ideas over longer distances and among larger groups of trading partners, other people become more valuable alive than dead, and they are less likely to become targets of demonization and dehumanization. *Feminization* is the process in which cultures have increasingly respected the interests and values of women. Since violence is largely a male pastime, cultures that empower women tend to move away from the glorification of violence and are less likely to breed dangerous subcultures of rootless young men. The forces of *cosmopolitanism* such as literacy, mobility, and mass media can prompt people to take the perspective of people unlike themselves and to expand their circle of sympathy to embrace them. Finally, an intensifying application of knowledge and rationality to human affairs—the *escalator of reason*—can force people to recognize the futility of cycles of violence, to ramp down the privileging of their own interests over

1943, and executed two years later.

others', and to reframe violence as a problem to be solved rather than a contest to be won.[17]

It is worth noting that precisely these forces are the ones targeted by right-wing political movements, as epitomized by the Trump administration, and so Pinker's warning that progress is not inevitable must be taken very seriously. However, we have now gone nearly seventy years without a conflict between major world powers, the longest such stretch since the Roman Empire. Hegel himself emphasizes the role of reason, ethical life, and the state in the actualization of freedom.[18] "Ethical life" includes aspects of what Pinker calls commerce, feminization, and cosmopolitanism. Hegel knows that constant vigilance is required to maintain ethical life, and that civilizations can and do regress.

Our present-day challenges to reduce violence are enormous—including irreversible damage to the environment, reckless governance (which makes the state an instrument of violence), racism, sexism, bigotry, terrorism, and the slaughter of innocents through nuclear war or semiautomatic weapons. Is our continuing struggle against violence a proof of God, of divine providence? I think only an essentially religious intuition of history can discern that. At the very end of his lectures on world history, Hegel writes: "What is important to discern is that spirit can find freedom and satisfaction only in history and the present—and that what is happening and has happened does not just come from God but is God's work."[19]

But do religion and divine providence really reduce violence? This is a topic for another book. The fact is that religion has often been a promoter of violence in history and not an instrument of

17. Pinker, *The Better Angels of Our Nature*, xxvi; see also 680–92. The biblical Leviathon is Thomas Hobbes's name for the political state. When scaled to world population, the Second World War is the ninth bloodiest contest in human history, and the First World War the sixteenth (195). Pinker's argument has been updated in his most recent book, *Enlightenment Now*.

18. Hegel has a philosophical (and theological) understanding of these factors, not a social-scientific one. But his views and Pinker's, while argued very differently, are not entirely dissimilar.

19. *Lectures on the Philosophy of World History*, 521.

peace. Pinker views it only in this negative aspect. I acknowledge that religion can be defrauded into an ideology used to justify hatred, arouse fear, or encourage violence against others; but that is false religion, not true religion. Such religion is not God's work but a mask of evil—a projection of the human ego, not an elevation to the divine that honors and glorifies God.

For Hegel "giving God the honor and glory" is an act of participation in the being and truth of God such that one's self-consciousness is the substantial consciousness of God, God's self-consciousness.[20] God's "glory" is simply the radiance of God's free being, its shining essence. God's glory is the ultimate meaning of freedom and the final end of world history, manifesting itself as the glorious freedom of the children of God (Rom 8:21) and the peace of God (Phil 4:7). This end is experienced repeatedly in history by both individuals and spiritual communities. It is a religious moment, but it has practical applications. The religious person is driven beyond the community into the world to work for its transformation by the actualization of freedom in ever-new but always fragmentary situations. We shape scenes of freedom in the midst of conflicting forces on the stage of history. We take two steps forward and one step back. The eschatological status is one of "already" and "not yet," and humans live in the tensive space between them. We should not look to a chronological or supernatural future for the consummation of history; it is happening here and now but is never fully attained. The way to the goal is no mere means but the goal itself, the thing that history is about.

---

20. Ibid., 168.

Writings by Peter C. Hodgson

Authored Books

Shapes of Freedom: Hegel's Philosophy of World History in Theological Perspective. Oxford: Oxford University Press, 2012.

Liberal Theology: A Radical Vision. Minneapolis: Fortress, 2007.

Hegel and Christian Theology: A Reading of the Lectures on the Philosophy of Religion. Oxford: Oxford University Press, 2005.

Christian Faith: A Brief Introduction. Louisville: Westminster John Knox, 2001.

Theology in the Fiction of George Eliot: The Mystery Beneath the Real. London: SCM, 2001. Minneapolis: Fortress, 2001 (with reversal of title and subtitle).

God's Wisdom: Toward a Theology of Education. Louisville: Westminster John Knox, 1999.

Winds of the Spirit: A Constructive Christian Theology. Louisville: Westminster John Knox; London: SCM, 1994.

God in History: Shapes of Freedom. Nashville: Abingdon, 1989.

Revisioning the Church: Ecclesial Freedom in the New Paradigm. Philadelphia: Fortress, 1988.

New Birth of Freedom: A Theology of Bondage and Liberation. Philadelphia: Fortress, 1976.

Children of Freedom: Black Liberation in Christian Perspective. Philadelphia: Fortress, 1974.

Jesus—Word and Presence: An Essay in Christology. Philadelphia: Fortress, 1971.

The Formation of Historical Theology: A Study of Ferdinand Christian Baur. New York: Harper & Row, 1966.

WRITINGS BY PETER C. HODGSON

Edited and/or Translated Books

Translator (with Robert F. Brown): *Ferdinand Christian Baur and the History of Early Christianity*. Edited by Martin Bauspiess, Christof Landmesser, and David Lincicum. Oxford: Oxford University Press, 2017.

Editor: Ferdinand Christian Baur. *Lectures on New Testament Theology*. Translated by Robert F. Brown Oxford: Oxford University Press, 2016.

Editor and Translator (with Robert F. Brown): Ferdinand Christian Baur, *History of Christian Dogma*. Oxford: Oxford University Press, 2014.

Editor and Translator (with Robert F. Brown): George Wilhelm Friedrich Hegel. *Lectures on the Philosophy of World History, vol. 1: Manuscripts of the Introduction and The Lectures of 1822-23*. Oxford: Clarendon, 2011.

Editor and Translator: Georg Wilhelm Friedrich Hegel. *Lectures on the Proofs of the Existence of God*. Oxford: Oxford University Press, 2007.

Editor and Translator: *G. W. F. Hegel: Theologian of the Spirit*. Minneapolis and Edinburgh: Fortress and T. & T. Clark, 1997.

Translator (with J. Michael Stewart): G. W. F. Hegel. *Lectures on Natural Right and Political Science: The First Philosophy of Right*. Berkeley, Los Angeles, London: University of California Press, 1995. Reissued by Oxford University Press, 2012.

Translator (with J. Michael Stewart): Walter Jaeschke. *Reason in Religion: The Foundations of Hegel's Philosophy of Religion*. Berkeley, Los Angeles, London: University of California Press, 1990.

Editor and Translator: Georg Wilhelm Friedrich Hegel. *Lectures on the Philosophy of Religion*. 3 vols. Edited by Peter C. Hodgson. Translated by Robert F. Brown, Peter C. Hodgson, and J. Michael Stewart. Berkeley, Los Angeles, London: University of California Press, 1984-1987. Vol. 1, *Introduction* and *The Concept of Religion* (1984). Vol. 2, *Determinate Religion* (1987). Vol. 3, *The Consummate Religion* (1985). One-volume edition: *The Lectures of 1827* (1988). Reissued by Oxford University Press, 2006 (one-volume edition), 2007 (three-volume edition).

Coeditor: *Readings in Christian Theology*. Edited by Peter C. Hodgson and Robert H. King. Philadelphia and London: Fortress and SPCK, 1985, 1994.

Coeditor and Coauthor: *Christian Theology: An Introduction to Its Traditions and Tasks*. Edited by Peter C. Hodgson and Robert H. King. Philadelphia: Fortress, 1982; London: SPCK, 1983. Coauthor of Chap. 2, "Scripture and Tradition," and Chap. 9, "The Church." 2nd edition, revised and enlarged, 1985. 3rd edition, updated, 1994.

Editor (with Introduction and Annotations). David Friedrich Strauss, *The Life of Jesus Critically Examined*. Translated by George Eliot. Philadelphia: Fortress, 1972; London: SCM, 1973.

Editor and Translator: *Ferdinand Christian Baur: On the Writing of Church History*. New York: Oxford University Press, 1968.

WRITINGS BY PETER C. HODGSON

Articles, Essays, and Book Chapters

"Life in the Spirit," in *The Oxford Handbook of Nineteenth-Century Christian Thought*, edited by Joel Rasmussen, Judith Wolfe and Johannes Zachhuber, 659–75. Oxford: Oxford University Press, 2017.

"Hegel and Baur," in *The T&T Clark Companion to Atonement*, edited by Adam J. Johnson, 537–42. London: Bloomsbury T. & T. Clark, 2017.

"F. C. Baur's Interpretation of Christianity's Relationship to Judaism," in *Is There a Judeo Christian Tradition? A European Perspective*, edited by Emmanuel Nathan and Anya Topolski, 31–51. Perspectives on Jewish Texts and Contexts 4. Berlin: de Gruyter, 2016.

"Idealist/Hegelian Readings of the Bible," in *The New Cambridge History of the Bible*, vol. 4, edited John Riches, 197–207. Cambridge: Cambridge University Press, 2015.

"Hegel and Secularization," in *The Persistence of the Sacred in Modern Thought*, edited by Chris L. Firestone and Nathan A. Jacobs, 352–71. Notre Dame, IN: University of Notre Dame Press, 2012.

"Hegel's Proofs of the Existence of God," in *A Companion to Hegel*, edited by Stephen Houlgate and Michael Baur, 414–29. Blackwell Companions to Philosophy. Oxford: Blackwell, 2011.

"Excursions into Difficulty." *Presbyterian Voices for Justice* website, October 2010.

"Liberal Theology." *Expository Times* 122:1 (October 2010) 4–10.

Articles on F. C. Baur, George Eliot, G. W. F. Hegel, Theological Concepts of History, Liberalism in Christian Theology and Ethics, in *The Cambridge Dictionary of Christianity*, edited by Daniel Patte. New York: Cambridge University Press, 2010.

"Luther and Freedom," in *The Global Luther: A Theologian for Modern Times*, edited by Christine Helmer, 32–48. Minneapolis: Fortress, 2009.

"Hegel's Philosophy of Religion." In *The Cambridge Companion to Hegel and Nineteenth-Century Philosophy*, edited by Frederic C. Beiser, 230–52. New York: Cambridge University Press, 2008.

"*Hegel and Christian Theology*: Author's Summary," and "Hegel: Theologian of Freedom." *The Owl of Minerva* 37 (Fall/Winter 2005-2006) 1–7, 71–82. This issue is devoted to a symposium on *Hegel and Christian Theology*.

"Christian Theology in an Age of Terror." *Witherspoon Network News* 25:1 (Winter 2005) 4–7; 25:2 (Spring 2005) 5–8. Also on the Witherspoon Society website.

"The Spirit and Religious Pluralism." *Horizons* 31 (Spring 2004) 22–39. Published in slightly different form in *The Myth of Religious Superiority: Multifaith Explorations of Religious Pluralism*, edited Paul F. Knitter, 135–50. Maryknoll, NY: Orbis, 2005.

"A Theologian of Mediation: Personal Reflections from Half a Century." *The Vanderbilt Divinity School Spire* 24:1 (Fall 2003) 14–18.

Writings by Peter C. Hodgson

"F. C. Baur, Theologian of History: Revisited after Forty Years." *Papers of the Nineteenth Century Theology Group* 34 (Eugene, OR: Wipf & Stock, 2003) 47-70.

"George Eliot's Religious Pilgrimage," in *Ethical Monotheism, Past and Present: Essays in Honor of Wendell S. Dietrich*, edited by Theodore M. Vial and Mark A. Hadley, 92-119. Providence: Brown Judaic Studies, 2001. Reprinted in *Creative Transformation* 15:2 (Spring 2006) 2-12, 34-41.

"Liberal Theology and Transformative Pedagogy." *Teaching Theology and Religion* 2 (June 1999) 65-76. A longer version of this essay is found in *The Future of Liberal Theology*, edited by Mark D. Chapman, 99-128. Aldershot, UK: Ashgate, 2002.

"Constructive Theology and Biblical Worlds," in *Teaching the Bible: The Discourses and Politics of Biblical Pedagogy*, edited by Fernando F. Segovia and Mary Ann Tolbert, 46-56. Maryknoll, NY: Orbis, 1998.

Coauthor, with Susan Brooks Thistlethwaite, "The Church, Classism, and Ecclesial Community," in *Reconstructing Christian Theology*, edited by Rebecca Chopp and Mark K. Taylor, 303-25. Minneapolis: Fortress, 1994.

"Providence," in *A New Handbook of Christian Theology*, edited by Donald W. Musser and Joseph L. Price, 394-97. Nashville: Abingdon, 1992.

"Ernst Troeltsch as Constructive Theologian," in *Papers of the Nineteenth Century Theology Working Group*, edited by Sandra Yocum Mize and Walter E. Wyman, Jr., 71-85. Colorado Springs: Colorado College, 1991.

"Roundtable Discussion: The Influence of Feminist Theory on My Theological Work." *Journal of Feminist Studies in Religion* 7 (1991) 110-12.

"Logic, History, and Alternative Paradigms in Hegel's Interpretation of the Religions." *The Journal of Religion* 68 (1988) 1-20.

"The Metamorphosis of Judaism in Hegel's Philosophy of Religion." *The Owl of Minerva* 19 (1987) 41-52. Reprinted in *Hegel Today*, edited by Bernard Cullen, 88-101. Aldershot, UK: Gower, 1988.

"Ecclesia of Freedom." *Theology Today* 44 (1987) 222-34.

"Alienation and Reconciliation in Hegelian and Post-Hegelian Perspective" *Modern Theology* 2 (1985) 42-63.

"Georg Wilhelm Friedrich Hegel," in *Nineteenth Century Religious Thought in the West*, edited by Ninian Smart et al., 3 vols., 1:81-121. Cambridge: Cambridge University Press, 1985.

"Hegel's Christology: Shifting Nuances in the Berlin Lectures." *Journal of the American Academy of Religion* 53 (1985) 23-40.

"Hegel's Approach to Religion: The Dialectic of Speculation and Phenomenology." *The Journal of Religion* 64 (1984) 158-72.

(with Leander Keck), "Christology: A Future?" *Religion in Life* 42 (1973) 8-24.

"Freedom, Dignity, and Transcendence: A Response to B.F. Skinner." *Soundings* 55 (1972) 347-58.

"Heidegger, Revelation, and the Word of God." *The Journal of Religion* 49 (1969) 228-52.

Writings by Peter C. Hodgson

"Karl Rahner," in *The New Day: Catholic Theologians of the Renewal*, edited by William Jerry Boney and Lawrence F. Molumby, 46-61. Richmond: John Knox, 1968.

"The Death of God and the Crisis in Christology." *The Journal of Religion* 46 (1966) 446-62.

"The Son of Man and the Problem of Historical Knowledge." *The Journal of Religion* 41 (1961) 91-108.

Review Essays

"*In Face of Mystery: A Constructive Theology* by Gordon D. Kaufman." *Journal of the American Academy of Religion* 62 (1994) 201-5.

"*Erring: A Postmodern A/Theology* by Mark C. Taylor." *Religious Studies Review* 12 (1986) 256-59.

"A Christology of Liberation": Review of *The Point of Christology* by Schubert M. Ogden. *Interpretation* 38 (1984) 302-5.

"Thinking the Being of God: The Recent Work of Robert Scharlemann." *Religious Studies Review* 9 (1983) 338-42.

"*Faith in History and Society* by J. B. Metz." *Religious Studies Review* 7 (1981) 31-33.

"G. W. F. Hegel, Religionsphilosophie, Band I: *Die Vorlesung von 1821*, edited by K.-H. Ilting (Naples: Bibliopolis, 1978)." *The Owl of Minerva*, 11/2 (1979) 4-7.

"*Theology and the Philosophy of Science* by Wolfhart Pannenberg." *Religious Studies Review* 3 (1977) 215-18.

"Towards a History of Nineteenth-Century Theology: A Review Essay." *Journal of the American Academy of Religion* 41 (1973) 591-96.

"Pannenberg on Jesus: A Review Article." *Journal of the American Academy of Religion* 36 (1968) 373-84.

"The Rediscovery of Ferdinand Christian Baur: A Review of the First Two Volumes of His *Ausgewählte Werke*." *Church History* 33 (1964) 206-14.

Numerous brief reviews in *Religious Studies Review* and other journals.

Forthcoming Editions (with Robert F. Brown)

Ferdinand Christian Baur, *Christianity and the Christian Church of the First Three Centuries*, and *Church and Theology in the Nineteenth Century*. Eugene, OR: Cascade Books, 2018, 2019.

Bibliography

Barth, Karl. *Church Dogmatics*. 13 vols. Various translators. Edinburgh: T. & T. Clark, 1936–62.
Baur, Ferdinand Christian. *Church and Theology in the Nineteenth Century*. Edited by Peter C. Hodgson. Translated by Robert F. Brown and Peter C. Hodgson. Eugene, OR: Cascade Books, 2018.
———. *History of Christian Dogma*. Edited by Peter C. Hodgson. Translated by Robert F. Brown and Peter C. Hodgson. Oxford: Oxford University Press, 2014.
———. *Lectures on New Testament Theology*. Edited by Peter C. Hodgson. Translated by Robert F. Brown. Oxford: Oxford University Press, 2016.
Bonhoeffer, Dietrich. *Prisoner for God: Letters and Papers from Prison*. Edited by Eberhard Bethge. Translated by Reginald H. Fuller. New York: Macmillan, 1953.
Calvin, John. *Institutes of the Christian Religion*. 2 vols. Edited by John T. McNeill. Translated by Ford Lewis Battles. Philadelphia: Westminster, 1960.
Chernow, Ron. *Grant*. New York: Penguin, 2017.
Cobb, John B., Jr. *Jesus' Abba: The God Who Has Not Failed*. Minneapolis: Fortress, 2015.
Ebeling, Gerhard. *Word and Faith*. Translated by James W. Leitch. New York: Harper, 1963.
Eliot, George. *Middlemarch*. Edited by Rosemary Ashton. London: Penguin, 1994.
Farley, Edward. *Divine Empathy: A Theology of God*. Minneapolis: Fortress, 1996.
———. *Ecclesial Man: A Social Phenomenology of Faith and Reality*. Philadelphia: Fortress, 1975.
———. *Ecclesial Reflection: An Anatomy of Theological Method*. Philadelphia: Fortress, 1982.
———. *Good and Evil: Interpreting a Human Condition*. Minneapolis: Fortress, 1990.

Bibliography

———. *The Transcendence of God: A Study in Contemporary Philosophical Theology*. Philadelphia: Westminster, 1960.

———. *Thinking about Things and Other Frivolities*. Eugene, OR: Cascade Books, 2014.

Forstman, H. Jackson. *Christian Faith in Dark Times: Theological Conflicts in the Shadow of Hitler*. Louisville: Westminster John Knox, 1992.

Frei, Hans. *Types of Christian Theology*. Edited by George Hunsinger and William C. Placher. New Haven: Yale University Press, 1992.

Hansen, Suzy. *Notes on a Foreign Country: An American in a Post-American World*. New York: Farrar, Straus & Giroux, 2017.

Hegel, Georg Wilhelm Friedrich. *Lectures on the Philosophy of Religion*. 3 vols. Edited by Peter C. Hodgson. Translated by Robert F. Brown, Peter C. Hodgson, and J. Michael Stewart. Berkeley: University of California Press, 1984–1987. Reissued by Oxford University Press, 2006–7.

———. *Lectures on the Philosophy of World History. Vol. 1: Manuscripts of the Introduction and the Lectures of 1822–3*. Edited and translated by Robert F. Brown and Peter C. Hodgson. Oxford: Clarendon, 2011.

———. *Phänomenlogie des Geistes*. Edited by Johannes Hoffmeister. Hamburg: Meiner, 1952. *Phenomenology of Spirit*. Translated by A. V. Miller. Oxford: Clarendon, 1977.

Hodgson, Peter C., and Robert H. King, eds. *Christian Theology: An Introduction to Its Traditions and Tasks*. Philadelphia and London: Fortress and SPCK, 1982. 2nd edition, revised and enlarged, 1985. 3rd edition, updated, 1994.

———, eds. *Readings in Christian Theology*. Philadelphia: Fortress, 1985.

Kierkegaard, Søren. *Fear and Trembling*, and *Repetition*. Edited and translated by Howard V. Hong and Edna H. Hong. Princeton: Princeton University Press, 1983.

King, Martin Luther, Jr. *I Have a Dream*. Foreword by Coretta Scott King. New York: Scholastic, 1997.

———. *Letter from the Birmingham Jail*. Foreword by Bernice King. San Francisco: Harper, 1994.

———. *A Testament of Hope: The Essential Writings of Martin Luther King Jr.* Edited by James Melvin Washington. San Francisco: Harper, 1986.

Larson, Erik. *In the Garden of Beasts: Love, Terror, and an American Family in Hitler's Berlin*. New York: Crown, 2011.

Lindbeck, George. *The Nature of Doctrine: Religion and Theology in a Postliberal Age*. Philadelphia: Westminster, 1984.

Luce, Edward. *The Retreat of Western Liberalism*. New York: Atlantic Monthly Press, 2017.

Luther, Martin. *The Freedom of a Christian*. In *Luther's Works*, 31:327–77. Edited by Harold J. Grimm. Philadelphia: Muhlenberg, 1957.

Maclean, Nancy. *Democracy in Chains: The Deep History of the Radical Right's Stealth Plan for America*. New York: Viking, 2017.

McFague, Sallie. *Metaphorical Theology: Models of God in Religious Language*. Philadelphia: Fortress, 1982.

———. *Models of God: Theology for an Ecological, Nuclear Age*. Philadelphia: Fortress, 1987.

———. *The Body of God: An Ecological Theology*. Minneapolis: Fortress, 1993.

Moltmann, Jürgen. *The Crucified God: The Cross of Christ as the Foundation and Criticism of Christian Theology*. Translated by R. A. Wilson and John Bowden. New York: Harper, 1974.

———. *The Spirit of Life: A Universal Affirmation*. Translated by Margaret Kohl. Minneapolis: Fortress, 1992.

———. *Theology of Hope: On the Ground and the Implications of a Christian Eschatology*. Translated by James W. Leitch. New York: Harper, 1967.

Niebuhr, H. Richard. *Christ and Culture*. New York: Harper, 1951.

———. *The Meaning of Revelation*. New York: Macmillan, 1941.

Niebuhr, Reinhold. *Faith and History: A Comparison of Christian and Modern Views of History*. New York: Scribner, 1949.

———. *The Irony of American History*. New York: Scribner, 1952.

———. *The Nature and Destiny of Man: A Christian Interpretation*. One-volume ed. New York: Scribner, 1949.

Patchett, Anne. *Commonwealth: A Novel*. New York: Harper, 2016.

Pinker, Steven, *The Better Angels of Our Nature: Why Violence Has Declined*. New York: Viking, 2011.

———. *Enlightenment Now: The Case for Reason, Science, Humanism, and Progress*. New York: Viking, 2018.

Ramsey, Paul. *Basic Christian Ethics*. New York: Scribner, 1950.

Robinson, James M., and John B. Cobb Jr., eds. *The Later Heidegger and Theology*. New York: Harper & Row, 1963.

———. *The New Hermeneutic*. New York: Harper & Row, 1964.

———. *Theology as History*. New York: Harper & Row, 1967.

Robinson, Marilynne. *Gilead*. New York: Farrar, Straus & Giroux, 2004.

———. *Home*. New York: Farrar, Straus & Giroux, 2008.

Schleiermacher, Friedrich. *Christian Faith: A New Translation and Critical Edition*. Edited by Catherine L. Kelsey and Terrence N. Tice. Translated by Terrence N. Tice et al. 2 vols. Louisville: Westminster John Knox, 2016.

Strauss, David Friedrich. *The Life of Jesus Critically Examined*. Translated by George Eliot. Reprint edited with an introduction by Peter C. Hodgson. Philadelphia: Fortress, London: SCM, 1972.

TeSelle, Eugene. *Augustine, the Theologian*. New York: Herder & Herder, 1970.

———. *Christ in Context: Divine Purpose and Human Possibility*. Philadelphia: Fortress, 1975.

Tillich, Paul. *The Courage to Be*. New Haven: Yale University Press, 1952.

———. *The Protestant Era*. Translated with a concluding essay by James Luther Adams. Chicago: University of Chicago Press, 1948.

———. *The Shaking of the Foundations*. New York: Scribner, 1948.

———. *Systematic Theology*. 3 vols. Chicago: University of Chicago Press, 1951–63.

Bibliography

Troeltsch, Ernst. *The Christian Faith*. Based on lectures delivered at the University of Heidelberg in 1912 and 1913. Foreword by Marta Troeltsch. Edited by Gertrud von le Fort. Translated by Garrett E. Paul. Minneapolis: Fortress, 1991.

———. *Christian Thought: Its History and Application*. Lectures prepared for delivery in England, 1923. Edited by Baron F. von Hügel. New York: Meridian, 1957.

Ullrich, Volker. *Hitler: Ascent 1889–1939*. Translated by Jefferson Chase. New York: Knopf, 2016.

Williams, Robert R. *Hegel on the Proofs and the Personhood of God: Studies in Hegel's Logic and Philosophy of Religion*. Oxford: Oxford University Press, 2017.

———. *Tragedy, Recognition, and the Death of God: Studies in Hegel and Nietzsche*. Oxford: Oxford University Press, 2012.

Wilmore, Gayraud S. *Black Religion and Black Radicalism: An Interpretation of the Religious History of Afro-American People*. 2nd ed. revised. Maryknoll, NY: Orbis, 1983.

Index

Abba, 47–52
Abelard, 85
abortion, 102
Acts of the Apostles, 80
Alexander, Lamar, 107
Angyal, Istvan, 65
Angyal, Sara Bubik Fornady, 62–65
Anselm, 85
Anton, Jennifer Anne Hodgson, 69, 72
Anton, Thomas C., III, 72
Apocrypha, 29n
audacity, 35–37
Augustine, 19, 74, 85

Baldwin, James, 110
Baltimore, 4, 59
Barmen Declaration, 77
Barth, Karl, 71, 77–78, 83–84, 93
Batey, Brenda, 72
Baur, Ferdinand Christian
   as historian of church and theology, 81, 98–99
   and the history of early Christianity, 101
   his interpretation and appropriation of Hegel, 82
   as New Testament scholar, 80, 100
   his relation to Strauss, Möhler, and Hegel, 101
   as subject of PCH dissertation, 67–68, 81
   translations of his works, 98–101
   being (*Sein*) and human being (*Dasein*), 85
Berlin, 27, 69, 70n, 90
Bethge, Eberhard, 62
black theology, 88
Bonhoeffer, Dietrich, 62, 69–70, 104, 113
Boston, 65
Brooks, David, 74, 109
Brown, Coleman and Irene, 34–35, 60–61
Brown, Robert F., 90, 97–99, 101
Bubik, Gabriella Toth and Lajos, 63
Budapest, Hungary, 62–64
Bushnell, Horace, 89

Calhoun, Robert, 79
Calvin, John, 13, 84
Camp Miniwanca, 59
Camp O-At-Ka, 62, 65
chance, 44, 50, 113
Christ, *see* Jesus Christ
Christ and culture, 78–79, 83
Christianity
   early, 101
   Jewish and Gentile, 81
   as life-process of God, 82–83

127

as a moral power or teaching, 100
and the religions, 92
as tragicomic, 92, 110
christology, 71
Civil War, 56, 106n
Clark, Amy, 65
Clark, Jack, 10
clash in moral-religious worldviews, 109
Cobb, John B., Jr., 47–50, 85, 98
Coleridge, Samuel Taylor, 89
commerce, 114
commonwealth, 48, 52, 110
communion (Lord's Supper), 6, 17–19
Cone, James H., 88n
confessional theology, 105
congregation, as participant in a conversation, 19–20
conservatism (political), 107, 109
contextualizing, 93
Continental Can Company, 4, 56, 58n
Corker, Bob, 107
correlation, method of, 75
cosmopolitanism, 114
Crafts, Frederick Sherwood, 55, 57, 71–72
Crafts, Verna Harris and Harry Kent, 56–58
creation and providence, 71; *see also* God, providence of
critical thinking, 76
cross, crucifixion, 27, 33, 101, 104–5, 112
culture, challenges of modern, 93, 103, 105
cunning of reason, 111–12
cynicism, 105

death, 27, 29–33, 34–37, 44, 73, 81, 100, 103, 104, 112
Dellbrügge, Georg and Sybille, 43–45, 66, 69

DeLoache, Charles and Marjorie, 7–9
demonic, 27
despotism, 107
dialectical theology, 77
Dille Cooperative Parish, 61
Donahue, John R., SJ, 70
Douglass, Frederick, 89

Eagles Mere, Pennsylvania, 4–5, 7–8, 28, 60–62, 71–72, 94
Ebeling, Gerhard, 69, 85–86
ecclesiology, 91–92
Enlightenment, 108, 114
environmental crisis, 23, 102, 115
Episcopal Church, 6, 72
eschatology (already and not yet), 116
ethical life, 112, 115
evangelical theology, 105

faith, 11, 21–22, 26, 31–33, 40, 75, 81, 87, 92, 109, 113
Farley, Edward, 70, 72, 86–88, 96
fascism, 109n, 110
feet, 42–46
feminine, feminism, feminization, 51–52, 103, 114
fire, 25
floods, 18
Fornady, Tibor, 62–63
Forstman, H. Jackson, 68, 72, 88
freedom
actualization of in history, 98, 115–16
of the children of God, 50, 116
of Christians, 11–14
divine idea of, 112
ethical, 111
let freedom ring, 10–15
new birth of, 88
new paradigm of, 91–92
perfect (divine), 98, 116
progress of the consciousness of, 98, 104, 113

shapes of, 92, 98, 111
structures and symbolics of, 89
Frei, Hans, 68, 78, 79, 83, 84
Fuchs, Ernst, 85
Funk, Robert W., 69, 85

Genesis, 20–21, 24
George Eliot, 89, 94–96
German idealism, 89
God
  as Abba (Father), 47–52
  as absolute spirit, 82–83, 104
  children of, 50
  as the companion who calls us forward, 50
  eternal life of, 73
  glory of, 116
  as ground of being, 75–76
  in history, 92
  as ideal factor in history (guiding, persuading, luring), 98, 103–4, 112
  as King (Monarch), 47–48
  and love, 52, 81
  as lover, beloved, love itself, 19
  masculine and feminine images of, 51–52
  not a magician, 103
  omnipotence of, 49
  participation in the being of, 116
  presence of, 40–41, 49, 86, 92, 95–96, 113
  in process, 95
  providence of, 22, 92, 95–96, 98, 104, 111–16
  purpose of, 50–51, 116
  source of novelty and freedom in our lives, 50
  as supreme ideality, 103–4
  the one who loves in freedom, 93
  tragedy taken up into the divine life and negated there, 104–5
  as triune, 82–83, 93
  as unconditional meaning, truth, liberality, 109
  and the world, 104
  good and evil, 111–13
Gore, Albert, Sr., 106, 107n
Gore, Al, Jr., 106
Gustafson, James M., 61, 79

Hansen, Suzy, 110
Harnack, Adolf von, 77, 89, 99
Harrod, Howard, 70, 72
Hart, Ray L., 68, 85
Hartt, Julian N., 61, 79
hearing, 38–41
Heartland, 48–49n
Hegel, Georg Wilhelm Friedrich
  and Christian theology, 96
  advance from Kant to Hegel, 104
  configurations of consciousness, 81–82
  God as absolute spirit, 82–83
  influence on Baur, 81
  Lectures on the Philosophy of Religion, critical edition and translation of, 89–90
  his philosophy of religion, 82
  his philosophy of world history, 97–98, 111–16
  role of reason, ethical life, and the state in the actualization of freedom, 115
  translation of writings of, 97
Heidegger, Martin, 85–86
history of dogma, 99–100
history
  differences resolved through ever-new mediations, 82
  fabric of (interweaving of human passions and divine idea), 98, 111
  in God, 92
  God's redemptive presence in without violating the

INDEX

historical fabric, 92, 95–96, 98, 104, 111–13
  governed by reason, 113
  as the ideal embedded in the real, 104
  interpretations of, 75
  as progress of the consciousness of freedom, 98, 104, 113
  purpose or goal of, 98, 116
  self-manifestation of God in, 83–84, 92
  as a slaughterhouse, 112–13
  violence in, 112–15
  way to the goal is no mere means but the goal itself, the thing that history is about, 116
Hodgson, David Andrew, 68, 72
Hodgson, Eva Sara Fornady
  birth and childhood of, 62–65
  college years, 65–68
  as language teacher, 67–68, 71
  marriage of, 67
Hodgson, Jack Edward, 3–6, 55
Hodgson, John George, 3–4, 58n
Hodgson, Mary Crafts, 5, 7, 55, 58
Hodgson, Peter Crafts
  birth and childhood of, 55–58
  college years, 59–61
  marriage of, 67
  political views of, 106–16
  seminary and graduate studies, 61–62, 67–68
  students of, 70–71
  teaching at Vanderbilt Divinity School, 68–71
  theological views of, 101–6
  theological writings of, 86–96
  work as an editor and translator, 89, 97–101
Hodgson, William Welch and Alice Jennings, 3, 58
Holocaust, 70n

human beings, 13–14, 22–23, 25, 30, 32, 41, 44, 50, 78, 85, 100, 104, 112
human rights, civil rights, 10, 13, 15, 106, 108
humility, 35–37
Hungary, 63–64
hurricane, 27

integration, 13–15
interpreting, 92–93

Jaeschke, Walter, 89–90, 97
Jesus Christ
  as agent of God in the world, 104
  as channel of the Spirit, 26–27
  his concept of God and God's kingdom, 48–49
  death of, 27, 33, 81, 101, 103, 104
  as extremist, 10
  as founder of Christianity, 100
  humility and audacity of, 36
  as incarnate Logos, 81
  his moral-religious teachings produce a revolution in human consciousness, 81, 100
  as normative paradigm of God in history, 104–5
  as paradigmatic shape of freedom, 92
  participation in, 11
  as presence of God in words and deeds, 86
  as teacher, 32–33
John, Gospel of, 5, 24, 26, 78, 80–81
Judaism, 80–81

Kaminski, Julie (Julia) Crafts, 55, 57, 71, 73
Kaminski, Paul G., 5n, 71
Käsemann, Ernst, 69
Keck, Leander E., 62, 70

Index

Kefauver, Estes, 106
Kennedy, John F., 106
Kierkegaard, Søren, 21, 32, 74, 89
King, Martin Luther, Jr., 10–15, 104
King, Robert H., 91
kingdom of God, 33, 40–41, 48, 79, 92
Kirschbaum, Charlotte von, 77
Kline, Debby Hodgson, 55
Küng, Hans, 69

Lake Balaton, 63
Landes, George and Carol, 59
Lawson, James, 68, 70, 88
Leverenz, David, 72
liberal democratic consensus, 107–9
liberal theology, 78–79, 109
liberalism (political), 106–7
liberalism (theological), 109
liberation theology, 71, 88–89, 92
life, 5, 11, 14, 18, 25, 27, 30, 32, 34, 37, 73, 98, 102–3
Lincoln, Abraham, 88
Lindbeck, George, 78, 79
Linders, Robert, 47
love, 10, 19, 45, 49, 52, 81, 93, 95
Luke, Gospel of, 10
Luther, Martin, 10–12, 69–70, 79, 85

MacLean, Nancy, 107
Magician Lake, 56–58
Mark, Gospel of, 30–33
Matthew, Gospel of, 45–46, 80
Maurice, Frederick Denison, 78–79
McFague, Sallie, 70, 86–87
Memphis, 4, 56–57
Meyer, Paul, 61, 79
Minear, Paul, 61, 79
miracle and supernaturalism, 102–3
Moltmann, Jürgen, 60, 86, 88–89

mortality, 37, 73
Mushroom Cottage, 4, 62, 71
mystery beneath the real, 95

Nashville, 18, 68, 71–72, 94, 106
Nazism, 27, 64, 77
New Frontiers in Theology, 85
new hermeneutic, 85
Niebuhr, H. Richard, 61, 78–79, 84
Niebuhr, Reinhold, 61, 74–75, 78, 84
nineteenth-century theology, 71, 89

Oak Park, Illinois, 4, 6, 55
Ogletree, Thomas, 70
Origen, 85

Pannenberg, Wolfhart, 85–86
parables, 24, 39–41
paradigm shifts, 91–92
Paris, Peter, 70
pastoral ministry, 16–23, 92
Patchett, Ann, 48
Paul, the Apostle, 80–81, 100–101
Pauline and Deutero-Pauline epistles, 80
Pennsylvania, 14, 61, 107
Peter, the Apostle, 80
Philadelphia, 3, 58n
Pinker, Steven, 114–15
politics, 106–16
Pratt, Jim and Nancy, 66, 68
Presbyterian Church, Presbyterianism, 11, 72, 85
Princeton University, 34–37, 59–60
process philosophy/theology, 47, 50, 92, 98, 112
Protestant principle, 72, 75–76, 91
Psalms, 24–25, 44
public good, 110

racism, 13, 57, 106, 110, 115

131

Index

Rahner, Karl, 71
reason, 11, 107–9, 111–14
Reformation, five-hundredth anniversary of, 69
relativity, 76
religion, and violence, 115
religion of the future, 95
responsibility, 22–23
resurrection, 30, 45–46, 86
revisioning, 91, 93
revisionist theology, 105
Ricoeur, Paul, 88–89, 92
right-wing politics, 107–9, 115
Robinson, James M., 85
Robinson, Marilynne, 16–23
Royce, Josiah, 89

sailing, 26, 93–94
salvation history, 92
salvation, 11–13, 23
San Antonio, 68
Sasser, Jim, 106
scenes of freedom, 92, 116
Schelling, Friedrich, 75, 81
Schleiermacher, Friedrich, 78, 81–82, 84, 87, 89
Schubert, Paul, 61, 67, 79
Scotland, 8
Scots Confession, 8–9
secular worldview, 102
segregation, 13–15, 57
sermon, 18–20
sexual orientation, 102
shapes of freedom, 92, 98, 111
Smith, Helen Jean Crider, 57
Smith, Kelly Miller, 70
speaking, 39–41
speculative theology, 83
Spirit, spirit, 19, 24–27, 41, 45–46, 50, 79, 81–83, 92–93, 97, 103–4, 112, 115
St. Louis, 58
state (political), 114
Stewart, J. Michael, 90

Strauss, David Friedrich, 80, 89–90, 101
Student Christian Movement, 60, 62, 65
summer, 28–29
superabundance, 95
Swallows and Amazons, 56
Synoptic Gospels, 30n, 80
Syracuse, 64–65

Taubes, Jacob, 81–82
tendency criticism, 80
Tennessee, 106–7
Tennessee Democratic Party, 106
Tennessee Republican Party, 106–7
TeSelle, Eugene, 70, 72, 86–88
theologies, 84–85
theology of freedom, 88–89
theology of history, 83–84, 92, 98, 111–13, 116
theology
    constructive/systematic, 71
    ideality in, 103–4
    as an intrinsically historical discipline, 83–84, 92
    as a kind of fiction, 96, 101
    realism in, 102–3
    and world religions, 71
Thomas Aquinas, 85
Tillich, Paul, 61, 71, 75–76, 84
Topography of Terror Museum (Berlin), 70n
tragicomic vision, 110
Trinity, 71; *see also* God, as triune
Trinity University, 58
Troeltsch, Ernst, 78, 84, 89, 92, 105
Trump, Donald, 107–9, 115
two steps forward, one step back, 46, 116

Ullrich, Volker, 109n
Union Theological Seminary, 35, 59, 61, 75

132

Index

United States, 110
University of Tübingen, 68–69, 86

Vanderbilt Divinity School,
  68–71, 85–89, 90, 96, 106n
Vilas, Skip, 60–61
violence, 102, 113–15

Wainer, Judith Hodgson, 55
water, 18, 25
Welch, Claude, 67, 78, 79
Wellesley College, 62, 65–66
Westminster Foundation, 60, 62
Whitehead, Alfred North, 50, 98, 104
Williams, Robert R., 96
Wilmore, Gayraud, 60, 88n

wind, 24–27, 92–93
winter, 107
Wisdom of Solomon, 28–30
Wittenberg Town Church, 70n
Word of God, 85–86
Workgroup on Constructive Theology, 90–91, 105
World Council of Churches work camp, 60–61
world, growing good of, 95–96
world history, philosophy of, 97–98, 111–16; *see also* history
Württemberg, 64

Yale Divinity School, 43, 46, 61–62, 66–68, 70, 76–79

www.ingramcontent.com/pod-product-compliance
Lightning Source LLC
Chambersburg PA
CBHW032231080426
42735CB00008B/801